D0170928

American
Drama in Social Context

Morris Freedman

WITH A PREFACE BY

Harry T. Moore

SOUTHERN ILLINOIS UNIVERSITY PRESS
Carbondale and Edwardsville

FEFFER & SIMONS, INC.
London and Amsterdam

Copyright © 1971, by Southern Illinois University Press
All rights reserved
Printed in the United States of America
Designed by Andor Braun
International Standard Book Number 0–8093–0526–7
Library of Congress Catalog Card Number 79–156787

To
Miss Marjorie Nicolson
alma mater

Contents

Preface

Morris Freedman, who is now chairman of the English Department at the University of Maryland, is an outstanding critic of the modern theater. An earlier book of his, The Moral Impulse: Modern Drama from Ibsen to the Present, was a welcome addition to the Crosscurrents/Modern Critiques series in 1967; it received notably good reviews and sold very well. We are now happy to present its successor.

Morris Freedman for some years taught at the University of New Mexico, and I first met him at a D. H. Lawrence conference which E. W. Tedlock, Jr., had arranged there; it was about 1964 or '65. Professor Tedlock, author and editor of several distinguished books about Lawrence, had brought to Albuquerque and Taos several workers in the Lawrence vineyard, including Professor Warren Roberts, Director of the Humanities Research Center at the University of Texas who is also Lawrence's bibliographer, as well as the English novelist David Garnett, who knew Lawrence and has frequently written about him. Among other events we had a panel session in which Morris Freedman was one of the participants at the speaker's table on the stage of the auditorium.

As the author of the widely read and provocative books, Confessions of a Conformist and Chaos in Our Colleges, he had a large following among the students

attending the session. The principal argument, as I recall, was about pornography and obscenity, not Lawrence's main line but an interesting sidetrack; Morris
Freedman, accompanied by wildly cheering encourage-
ment from the students, was against any censorship
whatsoever; some of the rest of us agreed with Lawrence
that there was really dirty dirt which should perhaps not
be licensed. It is a ticklish question, for if there is to be
any censorship we might well ask who the censor
would be.

We didn't solve the problem that afternoon, although we had a good deal of fun with it, and while
Morris Freedman's students weren't organized as a
claque, they had the effect of one. The rest of us were
able to get a word in once in a while when we could grab
the microphone, passed back and forth among those of
us at the table, and could hold onto that mike for awhile
while trying to present our own views. The students
shouted that we were "hogging the mike" and not let-
ting Morris Freedman say enough. Anyhow, we did have
fun.

And there's always fun in Morris Freedman, for he
writes nimbly and mischievously as well as deeply; he is
always stimulating to read. In the present volume he
deals chiefly with American dramatists of our time, including that longtime British citizen, the St. Louis-born
T. S. Eliot, whom he examines most interestingly as one
making an effort to cling to the shibboleths of what he
recognized as the élite tribe. Approaching Eliot from this
angle, Morris Freedman is able to make some effective
observations about his plays in general, at one point even
contrasting him with the always controversial Lawrence,
on this occasion in Lawrence's favor.

The book also contains a highly interesting chapter on
some of the most recent American dramatists, including
LeRoi Jones, who wrote that contemporary classic, Toi-

let. And the author has much that is valuable to say about the "new Senecanism." His range is wide, for while placing current American playwrights in perspective, he discusses in passing a number of dramatists from other countries, including Federico García Lorca, Harold Pinter, Ugo Betti, and others.

In the Preface to Morris Freedman's earlier book in this series, I regretted that he hadn't included a chapter on Eugene O'Neill, but fortunately he has put one into the present book, a brilliant discussion of the later plays. He also discusses O'Neill in the excellent concluding chapter on the efforts of recent playwrights to turn out an American tragedy. There is also a section on Arthur Miller, who seems to me the most overrated of American dramatists—in seeing performances of his plays and in reading them, I am always struck by their flatness: it seems to me that the language never brings them alive, and that they—

But I won't hang onto the mike any longer, Morris: it's yours.

HARRY T. MOORE

Southern Illinois University
April 6, 1971

Acknowledgments

The following chapters appeared in part or in whole and in different form in the following publications and are here reprinted with permission and with my thanks to the editors and publishers.

Chapter 2, "O'Neill's Moral Energy," in the April 1962 issue of *College English* under the title "O'Neill and Contemporary American Drama."

Chapter 3, "Mr. Eliot's Drama: His Jew and His Jazz Rhythms," in two parts in *The South Atlantic Quarterly*: "Jazz Rhythms and T. S. Eliot" in 51, No. 3, July 1952; and "The Meaning of T. S. Eliot's Jew" in 55, No. 2, April 1956.

Chapter 6, "Will Success Spoil the American Dramatist?" as chapter 6, titled "Success and the American Dramatist," in *American Theatre*, Stratford-Upon-Avon Studies, 10, ed. John Russell Brown and Bernard Harris, London, 1967.

Chapter 7, "Violence in the Modern Theater: Notes on the New Senecanism," in the *New Mexico Quarterly*, 37, No. 4, Winter 1968.

I am grateful to my teachers, my students, my colleagues, and the members of my family who, over the years of the writing of this book, have been thoughtful, kind, generous, properly admonitory, challengingly skeptical, and, in so many important ways, supporting and inspiring. My wife, Charlotte, was a patient and enthusiastic companion in years of theatregoing. I am especially fortunate to be an alumnus and a continuing and loving student of the university to whom this work is dedicated. Needless to say, all shortcomings here are stubbornly my own.

MORRIS FREEDMAN

College Park, Maryland
March 1971

American Drama in Social Context

1

Drama and Society Mid-Century and Before

American drama in our time, like so much drama before it, has not often in its intention, even less so in its achievement, been primarily a literary art. It has been a form of public entertainment, subject to the combination of demands and standards that characterize entertainment and business. As Shakespeare's drama had to compete for profits with bearbaiting and bullbaiting productions and the more sensational works of the rival companies, so American dramatists have had to compete with opera, concerts, ballet, vaudeville, the movies, minstrel shows, radio, television, baseball, football, tennis, and, when it ventured out of urban centers, with rodeos and country fairs. What showed up in a play, that is, the movements, the lighting, the music, the sets, and the costuming, was often as important as what was said. The *Ziegfeld Follies* were theatrical happenings virtually empty of literary content.

This is not to disparage American plays, in which so much more happens than the dramatization of a text, but simply to emphasize the character of that drama in its living form. Of all the literary arts, then, drama is the most social, the one most immediately responsive to the context from which it emerges and in which it appears. The idiom of drama, like the idiom of poetry, reflects complex systems of values and ambitions, it crystallizes shades and tones of evidence, it focuses for audiences a range of commitments, and simultaneously, always, insistently communicates with the less aware members of these audiences, instructing and edifying them in the current vocabulary of concerns, attitudes, activities, and of course language. In a sense, drama, even more than poetry, may be said to be untranslatable, that is, it remains fixed in the social foundation in which it is structured. Moses Hadas in his introduction to a collection of the comedies of Aristophanes in translation put it well in comparing the Greek texts to a Marx Brothers movie.

> Aristophanes wrote for a specific audience and occasion, and would have laughed at the thought that remote generations might be fingering his plays. At the level of physiological jokes, therefore, and those that approach the physiological in universality, all who share our common physiology can understand him well enough. But allusions to contemporary persons, events, or usages, special connotations of words, and, in a more general view, the intellectual bent of Aristophanic wit sometimes leaves us in the dark—just as reflections of contemporary life in our comedy would be lost on a Greek audience. An old movie has Groucho Marx's secretary say, when two men are waiting to see him, "Epstein is waxing wroth," and Groucho replies, "Tell Roth to wax Epstein." How many volumes of commentary would a Greek require to understand all of the joke, and how unfunny it would be after he had studied the commentary!

The style and the strategy of any drama are so peculiarly intertwined with the habits of thought and of existential coping of a particular people at a particular time in a particular place that it becomes finally a kind of archaeological fact in itself, a form of evidence if we can but determine the witness it bears.

It is a curiosity of American literary history that American drama before 1920 is not studied except by specialists. Anthologies of American literature to be used in college surveys normally do not include earlier dramatic works. Courses in American drama usually begin around 1920. The Broadway theatre, the off-Broadway theatre, university theatres, little theatre groups throughout the country rarely revive American plays written before 1920. Although curious, this fact should not be altogether surprising after we look at the character of earlier American drama, especially by contrast with European works of the same time. The drama of Ibsen and of Strindberg, for example, both very specifically Scandinavian, recorded a tendency in Western civilization more than it did any particular regional character. It was possible for George Bernard Shaw, living in England, to find Ibsen contemporary and applicable to his own work. American drama before O'Neill and the Provincetown movement, by contrast, spoke provincially, parochially, almost to itself. Writing in *Harper's Weekly*, in 1904, William Dean Howells put it as follows:

A certain range of American and English plays which I have lately been seeing seem to divide themselves, broadly, into two sorts quite according to their nationality: the domestic sort and the society sort. The distinction applies both to such realistic and fantastic satires as *The Admirable Crichton*, *Whitewashing Julia*, and *Candida*, and to such widely differing pictures of our own life as *The County Chairman*, *Her Own Way*, *Glad of It*, *Our New Minister*, and *The Other Girl*. The English plays have to do with man as a society man, both in the narrower and the wider sense, and the American plays have to do with man as a family man; and I hope that a little thought about them will confirm the main interest is the home, and that with the English the main human interest is society. But lest we should be unduly proud of our difference from the English on this point, I hasten to suggest that this is because in the narrower English sense we have no society, and if we have a great deal of home, it is because we are still almost entirely rustic in origin, and preponderantly simple in our conceptions of happiness. In the wider sense we certainly have society; and it is a defect of our playwrighting that it does not carry over from the home to humanity. Its interest does not live from man to man, but from men to women, and from women to men; it has no implications; its meanings are for the given time and place only.

Henry James, who strained so hard so long to write serious drama during the period Howells described, could never achieve in the theatre that detachment and objectivity which would bring his text close to a universality which a more than personally ambitious American drama needed to have. His fiction, in which, like his great Victorian predecessors, he could comment on character, motivation, and the moral complexity of events and relationships, allowed him the means to find himself in and associate himself with the great tradition of the European novel. His "inadequate vulgarity," a shortcoming of character which T. S. Eliot also was later to strain against, prevented him from shaping any appropriate form of discourse in the theatre.

No simple order presents itself to examine American dramatic literature other than chronologically, from around 1920 to the present. The temptation is great to consider this body of work in sequences of ten-year periods, not least because public events arranged themselves as signal posts around the turn of each decade: the depression of 1929; the preparations for World War II around 1940; the half-century division itself of 1950; the political assassinations and the riots of the sixties. The formulations seem so ready and so familiar that we can easily slip a playwright or a particular play into an immediately available slot. But the documents of the literature themselves, the plays, do not conform except artificially to such easy and ready arrangements.

The problem of finding a comfortable vantage point, a point of perspective, from which to view modern American drama is reflected in the variety of approaches that our drama critics and historians have assumed. Joseph Wood Krutch studied the American drama since 1918, in a book with that title, in terms of prominent individual dramatists and works, offering shrewd and concise appraisals of specific styles and tendencies. Krutch brought to the regular critic's need to offer immediate guides the academic virtue of historical perspective, attention to significant detail, and a sensitive awareness of potential. John Gassner approached the subject by way of themes, with essays that made sweeping and valuable formulations about the drama of American realism or about various attempts at tragedy; his all-embracing efforts, of course, were so monumental, so basic, that it is pointless to find in Mr. Gassner's approach some reductive formula. He was the great recorder, the great historian. His comprehensive, encyclopedic surveys, by their sweeping inclusiveness, suggested in their straining after exhaustiveness a kind of avoidance to study closely a particular phenomenon or problem, to pause and ruminate. George Jean Nathan and Stark Young, serious and uncompromising students of the theatre, were, professionally, literary men first, and as such, in their various degrees and modes of seriousness and richness of allusion, important observers of the transient scene. But their study of the theatre took the form of single short essays principally, their periodical reviews; we can derive a sense of the man from their several collections but no such organic sense of the scene they were reporting. Brooks Atkinson and Walter Kerr provide evidence more of what audiences expected during their tenure of critical office rather than a lasting sense of the dramatic scene itself.

In later years, Harold Clurman, himself a passionate, not to say Messianic participant in theatrical activities, and Robert Brustein, a professor, critic, drama school dean, and sometime Isaiah, have tried to suggest, in entirely different ways, some of the fundamental troubles in the American theatre, focusing closely on the particularities of internal symptoms that were sure to have finally alarming external results.

In short, the fragmentation and variety of critical and historical approaches, the straining to fashion appropriate rubrics, the attempts to assign American instances of social comedy or of tragedy to recognizable categories, whether derived from contemporary Europe or from older periods and other places, suggest the difficulty of easy analysis and classification. But the problem, of course, is more than one of taxonomy, of finding the appropriate major and minor classifications.

The total American dramatic enterprise exists, much like the Hollywood film industry, outside the serious world of literary endeavor. It has been a large club, in which writers, actors, critics, producers, theatre owners, and occasional backers live in a happy, conspiratorial camaraderie. It is often astonishing to the literary historian that there should be American dramatists, like American film and television writers, who are virtually unknown outside their particular craft. In the company of Shakespeare, Dryden, Chekhov, Ibsen, Shaw, Brecht,

Pirandello, all of whom wrote in several forms, American dramatists are, by and large, practitioners of a single talent. Yet the dramatic text, the possibilities for statement offered by the form of the play, in the course of sheer colloquy or with the benefit of music and dance, obviously attracts serious writers in America for the chance it offers of large audiences.

In the thirties, drama achieved a new seriousness and importance, not so much as an arena for traditional theatrical endeavor but as a forum for social commentary and protest. Drama was used very specifically in the way Harriet Beecher Stowe had used the novel, or seventeenth-century English pamphleteers had used the broadside. First in New York and then in Hollywood, the political activists of the decade, especially those who committed themselves to a party-line assignment, turned to dramatic forms to propel the revolution. Even so passionately dedicated a professionally theatrical enterprise as the Group Theatre found itself fusing its theatrical zeal with a social one; indeed, the very momentum of its revolutionary stage mission prompted the assumption of revolutionary political stances.

Perhaps because of this period of very narrowly channeled political expression, specific solutions applied to specific causes, American drama failed to take on truly large political issues, whether of history or of philosophy. We have not had a serious American political drama comparable to the works of Bertolt Brecht, Albert Camus, or Ugo Betti, no sustained examination of the moral complications of power, or of that large spiraling landscape lying between the lowest and the highest levels in society, certainly nothing like the intertwined national, political, human, and historical concern of Shakespeare's history plays.

Our plays about the making of presidents have been forms of social comedy, comedies of manners, even musical comedy, most nearly resembling the drawing-room encounters of English Restoration and Edwardian plays (and rarely, for that matter, embodying the raw, brutal, social commentary of, say, Wycherley, or the impotent, sad, verbal extravagance of Wilde). We have had no one who has tried seriously to work even in the modern tradition of Shaw, who provided one model after another for serious relevant modern statement. Our writers not altogether committed to a particular vision achieved their greatest successes incidentally, as in the documentary by-product of an Odets. We have managed to avoid or mask even the most obvious and the most immediate social problems, like those involving minority ethnic groups, for example, slowly but inevitably moving into the centers of American life. Although the social issue of the Negro was considered early—in 1909, for example, in a play called *Nigger*—most subsequent plays have dealt with very specific, journalistic events (judicial or mob lynchings), emotionally affecting, certainly, but always falling short of confronting, or imagining, some more fundamental, and momentarily less sharply disturbing, future problem, like socially approved miscegenation (an eventuality Shaw considered in *Back to Methuselah*) or the real possibility of a separatist movement in our time. Plays about the Scottsboro boys, about one or another lynching in the South, about the immediate consequences of a particular mixed marriage, do not propose the larger issues we may find in the works of Genet or of Brecht, Hochhuth, or Weiss. Only recently have there been any breakthroughs into territories that do not evoke as a terminal objective the stereotypes of Amos and Andy or of minstrel shows in other than their recognizable milieus. A similar evaluation may be sustained about the treatment of the Jew in American life. Other minority groups as well, like homosexuals and drug addicts, have also been neglected in their social or philosophical or symbolic import until well past mid-century. (The homosexual camaraderie so prominent in works of the twenties like *What Price Glory?* or *The Front Page* was strangely, uncannily honest in its intimation of an obscured area of American life, but it was too oblique, too little self-aware, to suggest, say, the lines of connection with the grim social comedies of George Kelly.)

What voice has the American dramatist been trying to develop as he moved into maturity? What idiom, what style of discourse? The social drama of the twenties, thirties, and forties had an aggrieved tone, petulant, whining, the whimper of innocents confronting, for the first time perhaps, the familiar enough realities of the old world. Some social playwrights, like O'Neill and Kelly, to be sure, approached their subject matter more stolidly, more acceptingly, but with the similar openness of a naïve vision. In *Craig's Wife* and *The Show-Off*, Kelly was able, as a consequence of a noncommitted, disinterested concern with the manners of an emerging bourgeois domesticity, to apply that same sort of phenomenological insight marking the work of fictionists like Lewis and Dreiser and essayists like Mencken. O'Neill, absorbed by self but his perspective enlarged by that period of retreatlike omnivorous reading enforced by sanitarium confinement, mined his own experience and awareness in the forms of Scandinavian and German expressionism. The classical tension between the country and the city, recorded for the modern world perhaps most movingly for the first time by William Wordsworth in "Michael," O'Neill recorded and alluded to over and over again, as in *Anna Christie* and in *Desire under the Elms*. The bucolic, entirely private, isolated self-satisfaction of long periods of physically exhausting work, O'Neill sensed, marked one of the traumatic attacks on the individual of modern industrial America:

the tragic, final feeding on himself of Ephraim Cabot had the deepest, the best and the worst, puritanical roots, as much as Yank's similar self-destruction, in *The Hairy Ape*, the boiler-room stoker as proud of his feats of physical achievement as the farmer.

As the simpler aesthetic and polemical possibilities in the theatre were explored and then exhausted, as the social battles were finally won or lost, or, at least, settled somehow for the moment, dramatists began to turn to complexities more specifically literary in character. O'Neill, of course, kept experimenting, kept trying to force alchemical changes in the material itself he worked with, hoping thereby to achieve new statements of substance. But he worked his way, in a manner of speaking, back to Aristotelian first principles in his great work, *Long Day's Journey into Night*. Arthur Miller's progress as a playwright is more characteristic of the scene: we need only contrast *All My Sons*, a stiffly controlled exercise in the style of Ibsen, with *Death of a Salesman*, with its extremely complicated, fluid, flexible dramaturgic structure, moving across space and time, very nearly musical in its handling of theme and statement, to recognize how impelled American drama felt to move toward a richer artistic texture. The most serious of our great figures worked not only to resolve problems of substance, of subject matter and characterization, but also to settle problems of form. O'Neill, Rice, Miller, Albee all groped simultaneously to resurrect old forms, which would have the novelty of the old-fashioned and forgotten, and to shape new forms. T. S. Eliot, not first a dramatist, certainly one of the most responsive literary figures of any age, could at least attempt, if not achieve, a dramatic idiom that came as close as anyone else's efforts, in works like *Sweeney Agonistes* and *Murder in the Cathedral*, to suggest something of the feel and tone of the common world, even in his handling of the theme of ambivalent martyrdom in *Murder in the Cathedral* with its modern vulgar shadings. But his attempt is, finally, predominantly literary;. for all of its theatrical possibilities, *Sweeney Agonistes* has been rarely performed except as an academic curiosity or intellectually fashionable exercise.

The wrestling with form suggests the difficulty American dramatists have had in finding viable modes for their statements; it even hints at the difficulty in finding a suitable subject matter. Until the sixties, indeed, most American dramatists borrowed freely from continental writers. It is perhaps only in blending the possibilities of various peculiarly American media, film and television and vaudeville, that our manner may begin to affect foreign writers. Some important American plays, Albee's *The Zoo Story* and Kopit's *Indians*, received their first performances and recognition on the other side of the Atlantic.

One of the few authentic native styles, the slapstick verbal excesses of George S. Kaufman and his collaborators, and of S. J. Perelman, did not achieve their full serious dramatic possibilities until they were absorbed by some of the vaudeville absurdists of the sixties. The comfortable stability reflected in the social comedy of Pinero, Henry Arthur Jones, Maugham, or Coward never did seem properly American although their uneasy manner of old-world cynical brightness was the ambition of our social writers. But Americans had to invest the formal minuet with some redeeming social revelation, comment, or message. As a consequence, the well-made American comedic structure of Kaufman, the high-toned sophisticated world of S. N. Behrman, incorporate some element of fantasy, of wish fulfillment more than of observation; by contrast, Philip Barry's ambiguous world, the sleazy contexts of Robert Sherwood, the neurotic landscapes of George Kelly, suggested the truer nature of middle-class American life, something which is perhaps more visible to us from a distant perspective than it was at the time. The point is that Kaufman and Behrman registered the filtered view. The neatness, the comfortable sense of form, the resolution, the neatly polished and balanced phrases and exchanges, the satisfactions of problems posed and solved, all of these represented noble American social ambitions quite at variance with chaotic, malformed, prickly actualities. It has taken the aesthetic and textual confusions of an Edward Albee, the outrageously campy exercises of a Michael McClure, in *The Beard,* the pastoral perversity of Rochelle Owens, in *Futz!* to accept more capaciously, more curiously the difficulties, in communication and in statement, the strainings, the moral conflicts, of American life and bring them more nearly full surface. Robert Brustein spoke acutely in calling Jean-Claude van Itallie's play, *Motel,* a *metaphorical* distillation of American life in the mid-sixties.

Writing in *Harper's Magazine,* some fifty years after William Dean Howells, Robert Brustein tried to account for the fact that American plays were "not literature."

> As a consequence, American drama often seems to be the most mindless form of legitimate culture since eighteenth-century sentimental comedy, a form to which it bears more than a little resemblance . . . Our serious drama is informed by a debased Freudianism, our comedies are set in motion by man-chasing women, and our musicals—with one or two exceptions like *West Side Story* and *My Fair Lady*—are produced by people who write about Love while thinking about Money.

If the American theatre is to move into a new domain of effort, certainly the work of critics and theoreticians like Robert Brustein himself will be most helpful, perhaps actually essential. American drama, like other forms of American popular culture, has lacked a body of serious aesthetic criticism. It has only been at mid-century that serious, thoughtful, innovative thinkers about such subjects have emerged. American drama, it is beginning to be recognized, is sufficiently responsive and sensitive a medium to absorb all sorts of techniques of discourse—the work of nightclub monologists, of vaudeville and burlesque comedians, of improvisations on all levels of sophistication, of a mixture of mediums, in short, of all of the new and sometimes awkwardly ambitious efforts that have been so common in all of our forms of communication.

It is perhaps overoptimistic to expect that much vitality, certainly much that is dynamic and provoking in originality, will come from most academic theatrical enterprises, which, for all of their seeming "integrity" and freedom from the need of showing a profit, simply follow the lead of Broadway. Most academic or little theatre groups hardly trouble about reading new texts themselves, but they do read the annual volumes of Broadway's successful plays and the pronouncements of the *New York Times* drama man. The one striking exception, of course, is the revitalized Yale School of Drama, which combines a solid sense of the history and literature of drama with the driving energy of such enterprises as Blau and Irving's early San Francisco activity or Guthrie's Minneapolis one. Certainly, the revolutions in direction introduced by Tom O'Horgan (in such varied enterprises as *Hair, Tom Paine, Futz!*), the textual experiments of Arnold Weinstein, Jean-Claude van Itallie, Michael McClure, guerrilla theatre and street theatre, the whole new domain of black drama, provide a body of evidence that American drama has broken through restraining walls into strange and potentially rich new territories.

An authentic, an achieved, a uniquely American drama

will be born, if it has not already begun to show signs of birth, as the dramatic artists of all types in our culture confront the total American experience not only in its topographical reality, the sheer facts of the matter, but strain also to indicate the undertows, the more gnarled inner plumbing, those national qualities which, like it or not, we must acknowledge as our own—warts, wounds, heroic failures, and all.

2

O'Neill's Moral Energy

American drama in mid-century still has only one figure whose place is firmly alongside that of the great men of European drama: Eugene O'Neill. Perhaps one of the problems of American playwrights—and of some American critics and academicians—is their failure to evaluate properly O'Neill's achievement. Much of American drama lies in his shadow, but we have pretended that he is not there, or, at best, should not be there. O'Neill seems somehow too crudely, obviously American.

It is instructive to look at essays and histories of modern American drama. We can make an anthology of the casual dismissals, or of the grudging acceptances, of O'Neill, including the comments of critics like Krutch and Nathan who do acknowledge his greatness. O'Neill's restless experimenting, his grotesque melodrama, his overwriting, his lack of neatness and definitiveness as to theme or subject matter are immediately apparent. Eric Bentley's indictment and praise in his famous essay, candidly entitled "Trying to Like O'Neill," are in the tradition of Krutch's summation. The criticism adds up to saying that O'Neill never knew just what it was that he wanted to do or wanted to say. He said too much and he said it awkwardly. Lionel Trilling, in 1937, did grant to O'Neill the need to find his own philosophical center and suggested the moral energy that impelled all of his work. But for a long time Trilling remained almost alone in recognizing this essential quality in O'Neill. O'Neill defies any monistic critical placing; he defies any confident aesthetic or social evaluation.

Yet the fact is that O'Neill remains in the landscape, firmly rooted. Shakespeare, too, we recall, went through periods of being neglected or patronized. We always kept coming back to him. So do we always seem to keep coming back to O'Neill, whether as a result of stage or film productions of his work or because of a critic's need once again to define O'Neill's place or character. John Henry Raleigh's essay in *Partisan Review* examining O'Neill's Irish Catholicism in relation to the plays, for example, is an astute and most enlightening attempt to see O'Neill in the context of biography. The reappraisals of Kenneth Tynan and Lionel Abel, the full-length critical study by Raleigh, the ambitious biography by the Gelbs, the renewal of his early appreciation by Krutch, the recent collections of criticism by John Gassner and by others, add up to a virtual revival. O'Neill haunts us.

And rightly so, for O'Neill's essential quality is a seriousness that insists on confrontation. His moral energy is so intense and so dominating we quite forget about lesser questions, like style, plot, even characterization. Mary McCarthy comes to sneer at O'Neill's failure as a "writer," but she remains to consider solemnly the total effect of any particular work. A *Moon for the Misbegotten*, she concludes, "exacts homage for its mythic powers, for the element of transcendence jutting up woodenly in it like a great homemade Trojan horse." O'Neill's technical range, of course, is large, but whether he is writing expressionistic plays or naturalistic ones, whether he is concerned with an individual's relation to the world around him or with the tensions among the members of a family, he is merciless in raising universal questions. Whatever momentary descents to sentimentality there may be in O'Neill, he does not descend to sentimentality in the largest dimension of the play. O'Neill's granitic hardness about ultimate issues is what finally makes him impossible to escape.

Consider *Desire under the Elms*. It defies easy analysis as a tragedy. And perhaps it is not in any usual sense a tragedy, but this is not the point. The hero is heroic because, in spite of any inherent flaw, in spite of the world's arrangement of things to afflict him, he emerges triumphant. The loss of his wife, the loss even of his infant son, affirms him in his rocklike loneliness, strength, survival, and dedication. Perhaps this distresses us, too, for Ephraim has indeed given up something of that recognizable human frailty which makes us all, for the moment, Oedipus or Hamlet or Strindberg's captain.

Where O'Neill's emphasis is on Ephraim Cabot, Tennessee Williams's handling of a similar familial situation would have focused on the sons, or might have made the strength of Cabot like that of Kowalski, essentially animallike. Williams's *The Glass Menagerie* is as merciless a family portrait as O'Neill's *Long Day's Journey into Night*. But the characters, every one, of *The Glass Menagerie* are driven by self-pity, are focused almost pathologically inward; those of *Long Day's Journey* mesh with one another, feel one another's anguish and loneliness and share one another's fate. O'Neill's tragedy is familial, and consequently social, and ultimately universal; that of Williams is a mingling of several individual despairs and frustrations. It rarely rises above the clinical. O'Neill jars while Williams only puzzles, leaving all sorts of mysterious motives to hang like loose threads around the borders of his fabric.

O'Neill, like Faulkner, examines in the puritan context of American life such abominations as prostitution, adultery, alcoholism, dope addiction, near incest. He is a dark writer. But the examination is always in terms of finding a meaning, a form of understanding; the responsibility of one person to another is part of what makes the tragedy; O'Neill's tragic characters do not simply apologize for what they are, for what they have done; they seek to be understood or excused or forgiven, by themselves not least; they seek to find themselves in a mysterious world while still retaining their identity, while still assimilating their transgressions. Williams's characters are either arrogantly indifferent to the moral issue altogether, free-floating and unbound (Kowalski), or are shabbily sorry for themselves (Tom Wingfield). And, finally, Williams sometimes reads like a caricature of O'Neill: compare the fat old goat, Big Daddy, who lives on little but the memory of his lusts, with the truly huge figure of Ephraim Cabot. (Burl Ives, playing both roles in the films, accentuated the suggestion of burlesque.)

O'Neill cannot diminish his power even by his most excessive prolixity. If *The Iceman Cometh* had been written earlier in O'Neill's career, before every word of his became like every word of Shakespeare's, too precious to delete or change, it might conceivably have been edited as it progressed toward production, made shorter, tightened, focused. It might of course be argued that its very length and discursiveness, its seeming aimlessness, is necessary to its sheer physical impact of exhaustion. We are forced to empathize with the characters in virtually everything except the effects of alcohol: we feel as trapped in the theatre—or in the text—as the men do in the saloon. In this respect, *Iceman* preshadows the later American theatre of violence, in which the audience is assaulted, in a point-for-point equivalence, by the stage action: the "documentary" effect blurs with the aesthetic one. *Iceman* has a force and a validity that raise it above Saroyan's sentimental, engaging, but finally shallow skit of saloon life in *The Time of Your Life*. More than this, a careful reading of the text (as opposed to a viewing of the play which calls for an unnatural endurance) suggests affinities with the panoramic explorations of Strindberg in *A Dream Play* or *The Ghost Sonata*.

O'Neill stands as a point of reference, as a touchstone for American drama. *Death of a Salesman*, for example, like *Long Day's Journey*, is an account of the disintegration of an American family. We have two sons in each who cannot find themselves. In each, the husband suffers from a peculiarly deluding form of the American dream. The wives in each are fragile women, respected and loved by their men. Once we leave the superficial resemblances, however, the plays are poles apart. We know what it is that Tyrone "sells," what it is that has driven him to his compulsive investing in real estate to the neglect of his wife's and son's health. We understand how it is that his sons have remained so dependent on him. By contrast, we are asked to take the tragic events in Miller on faith and are persuaded to do so by an enormously skilled dramaturgy. But we see and feel that O'Neill's family carries its doom simply from being human beings with a particularized history. As in all tragedy, we are not asked or compelled by the playwright just to feel sorry for them. We identify. The fate of the Tyrones is the fate of all of us. The fate of the Lomans is ours only at stray moments.

O'Neill serves similarly to reveal the essential inadequacies of other American playwrights, Inge and Odets, Anderson and Hellman, Sherwood and Behrman and Wilder. *Our Town* is illustrative. It is an unflagging exercise in a whimsical avoidance of depth and particularity, especially in the reaching for "universality." It is not even quite like old *Saturday Evening Post* covers, which occasionally did portray a character with an individualized homeliness. Wilder's technique is like that of our shrewdest popular entertainers, to offer a joke, for example, while denying responsibility for it: if it is successful, the entertainer gets the applause; if it fails, well, it's not his fault, it's the fault of the joke. "This really happened . . ." is the gambit of these comedians; blame reality, blame truth, blame the plainness of American life, if the joke or the play doesn't come off. So with *Our Town*. If it is hackneyed, sentimental, indifferent to frustration and sadness (the town drunk; even the deaths of some of the main characters), well, that's life, you know: it really happened. By contrast, think only of *Ah, Wilderness!*, which is imaginative, lighthearted, summer-toned, yet never a superficial or generalized exploration of the same sort of context as that of *Our Town*. Although it suggests an idyllic reshaping of memory, or possibly of the fulfillment of a dream, it does not avoid confronting and honestly assimilating such common American horrors as alcoholism and an adolescent first encounter with sex. In the midst of the full family life, we are confronted with the sadness of frustration and escape of bachelordom and spinsterhood. O'Neill has the courage of his vision and does not need to use tricks to hedge his sense of rightness. (Compare, too, the easy and often imitative experimentalism of *The Skin of Our Teeth* with the original if awkward experiments of O'Neill.)

One of the more striking aspects of *Ah, Wilderness!* is its self-conscious, determined literary character. The encounters, the brushes, with literature, from the ancient world through the English romantic poets to the contemporary works of Shaw and Ibsen, suggest that O'Neill may, like so many other straining intellectual Americans of the twenties, have been reaching for an identification in the broad stream, the continuum, of the world's literature. The play is not merely about a young man showing off his learning; the literary references, like the literary background of *Mourning Becomes Electra* or that of James Joyce's *Ulysses*, provide a level of understanding, a kind of subsurface skeletal structure, a key to responding to the material, of making the immediate vitality of adolescent love assume a dimension and an energy larger than that of the passing moment. This unabashedly direct technique of O'Neill, to do the obvious heavy-handedly and without shading, works here as elsewhere. The strokes are thick and somewhat graceless; the colors are campy and unsubtle; virtually nothing in the play is new. Yet the drama works.

As always in O'Neill, the characters, their speeches, their total situation add up to persuade us against our smaller doubts. We do believe in the shallow, prattling, weak-willed, irrationally protecting mother; we do believe in the fumblings and the posturing of the adolescent boy; these are familiar yet special people. Perhaps more to the point, in understanding O'Neill in relation to the larger America in which he worked, is the note of poignant wishfulness which dominates the play. It is a play that would like to be about summer; it has almost a mythic yearning to be about just that season (one thinks about Northrop Frye's metaphoric use of the seasons in his criticism). The play may not have recorded an honest fact of recollection, particularly if we take *Long Day's Journey* to be more nearly autobiographical; yet the yearning that is recorded in *Ah, Wilderness!* is certainly itself honest, for we are persuaded by it and touched.

It is tempting to consider Eugene O'Neill's *Ah, Wilderness!* in terms of its relation to such earlier works as *Desire under the Elms* or to such later ones as *Long Day's Journey into Night*, all three about families in which there are at least two sons. All three plays, additionally, have a puritan focus, in their straining after wealth, after various forms of propriety, in their subdued passion, in the endless awareness of guilt in some shape or other.

Ah, Wilderness!, however, has a claim to being considered in its own and rather special right, and not simply because it is called a comedy. By comparison with other comedies of American domesticity, like those involving Booth Tarkington's *Penrod*, for example, or F. Hugh Herbert's skits, *Ah, Wilderness!* is very nearly black in the most contemporary sense. One of its striking scenes is an encounter between a newly graduated high school senior and a prostitute. It is funny, of course, but it is also poignant as it gropes through extremely sensitive areas involved in growing up, areas still rawly evocative even after the mid-century sexual liberation. The characters speak their scenes properly; they do not overstep the limits of expectations, given the situation, in terms of character and possibility; they are aware of the implicit disasters and, indeed, refer to them, and yet do not plunge into them. Alcoholism is a specter in the play both of terror and of comedy. Possibly the funniest scene, if "fun" is quite the word ever to use with an O'Neill situation, is that involving Sid Davis, in an improvised monologue growing out of an alcoholic inspiration.

Social plays like *The Hairy Ape* and *Anna Christie* are closer to the essential mysteries of American life than some of Odets's plays, for all of O'Neill's maudlin and pretentious details. Odets's work, of course, will always remain an authentic record, if only in stray speeches, of a significant part of American life. But Yank's quest for identity in an alien world, Chris's effort to find order and meaning for his daughter in the face of the world's fog and indifference, cut through to the essence of tragedy. Even those ambitious "Jamesian" studies of individual relations, in *Strange Interlude* and *Mourning Becomes Electra*, are more compelling and ambitious than Lillian Hellman's plays with a similar intent. At least, we cannot so easily say of O'Neill that he is Chekhovian or Ibsenian or, even, Strindbergian; he is characteristically himself, even when this is bad.

O'Neill's effort in the American theater has been a wide-ranging one. Like Faulkner, if he had not written so much and attempted so many different things, he would perhaps have not written his masterpieces. We may charge him with awkwardness, with lack of proportion, with a too sprawling ambition, with a failure to see the clear line between melodrama and tragedy, with lapses into uncomfortable sentimentality, with an incapacity to see and apply the point of technical experiments. We can never charge him with frivolity, with sheer imitation, with shallowness, with aimless theatricality.

O'Neill was engaged throughout his career in a challenging of the meanings and satisfactions of life itself. He offered answers gropingly and tentatively, never simply committing himself to any one course. O'Neill, like Faulkner, James, and Melville, spoke the American idiom with depth and involvement. He "engaged" with life. Like Faulkner and Hemingway, O'Neill deemphasized mind, for he felt and apprehended better than he could think.

And it is the seriousness of O'Neill's concern with his material, in theme, substance, and technique, which makes his body of drama finally as important as that of the European masters. Our other writers, however momentarily successful in defining significant issues (Sherwood, Behrman, Odets, Hellman, and Miller must be acknowledged to have had much to say of importance), our other writers have not been driven by that dedicatcd intensity to say as much in so many ways on so many issues—even when their voices at one moment or another were sharper and more clear. O'Neill reached out restlessly, even when he had no voice, even when his reaching was more like a blind, pathetic clutching, when he did not know just what it was he was reaching for. O'Neill's dramatic efforts were never the result of simple personal statement or apologia; personal understanding, yes, an understanding that in its depth and honesty transcended autobiography and became tragedy, that is, became an account of the human passage through life. *Long Day's Journey*, more than any play of O'Neill's, crystallized his power, written, as it was, as he said, "in tears and blood."

Long Day's Journey was published posthumously. It was written close to the end of his career, is plainly autobiographical, and was not intended for publication during his lifetime. It is perhaps all the more remarkable, then, that it is dramaturgically one of the tightest of his plays. It is not so loose and rambling, so verbose, as *The Iceman Cometh*, written for production. *Long Day's Journey* is neoclassically conventional: one setting, one compact period of time. We concentrate on the four members of the Tyrone family. The cook is never seen, reminding us, hauntingly, of the vampirish cook in Strindberg's *The Ghost Sonata*. A sense of doom pervades the action; symbols emerge: the fog that enshrouds the landscape; the lust for land, for rootedness, of the father; the mother's nostalgic return to her wedding gown; the consumption eating up Edmund.

But the dramaturgy neither in scope nor in detail accounts for the impact of the work, which combines documentary study with controlled art. Trauma mingles with purgation. We start with a microcosm, a shabby summer cottage housing a family, insulated from the world by the fog. The focus is intensely clinical; we move from the bright sunlight of the external world (emphasized in the spacious, light-filled opening scenes of the film) more and more narrowly into a surgical circle of light, in the progression laying bare past and present, deeper and deeper layers of agonies. A vague terror underlies the most obviously naturalistic or expressionistic surface. In *Anna Christie*, the man who comes to take Anna back to the world rises out of the sea; in *The Emperor Jones*, the hero drums himself back to savagery; in *The Hairy Ape*, Yank moves atavistically backward to an attempted identity with the zoo gorilla.

In *Long Day's Journey*, the characters, confronted with themselves, with each other, begin the sustained attempt to define and characterize themselves, with excruciating self-honesty. The dope addiction of the mother, the alcoholism of the father and his two sons, heighten and justify the tortures they visit on one another. In the final act, which vacillates between macabre humor and grotesque tragedy, all four characters have long ago left the territory of sobriety: they live in memory, they live in their desires, they live in the baring of lusts, weaknesses, jealousies, and affections. Ephraim Cabot's hardness put off his sons; they leave for the softness of California. Here, at last, the harsh landscape softened by time and a conspiratorial sharing of the analgesia of alcohol and dope, father, mother, and sons talk out their careers as mortal men and as family personages: we see James Tyrone alone and as a husband and father; we see the brothers isolated and then intertwined. Only the mother floats away, out of the family. The cruelty of the blunt speeches and confessionals is a tenderness of final intimacy, the compassion of the surgeon, the forced assumption of ultimate and necessary honesty.

The four persons do more than merely participate

in plot, of course. They represent forces, vectors, that move outward from the centrality, the centripetal familial power. James stands for a harsh, cynical, almost morbid "truthfulness," that, like the insistence on truth of the townspeople in Pirandello's *It Is So!* (*If You Think So*), is finally petty and monstrously untrue in the face of important, protective lies. There is a sickness in James Jr.'s obsessiveness with truth; he is impelled by hatred and jealousy, and knows this, can say so, and cleanses himself while he immolates himself. Edmund has sought nirvana in nature, finds it momentarily again in a flight of memory, knowing at last that he cannot soar away; he is sunk like so much leaden dross by his disease, by his familial identity.

It is James Tyrone, the father, who carries the heaviest symbolic weight, as he carries the greatest guilt, the greatest responsibility, the greatest burden of "tragic flaw." His miserliness, his compulsive real estate purchases, have become lustful, an energy directed toward a form of material immortality, a desperateness in trying to wipe out the insecurity of his awful childhood, when he became the head of a family at the age of ten. He knows all this, he says all this, and yet he cannot, for all his normal human affection, satisfy the needs of simple mortality, the needs, first, of his wife, then of his son, for decent medical attention. He is as willful as Lear in railing against reality. Death or disease or dope addiction cannot become as compelling for him as the threat of poverty, of landlessness. Real estate—as distinguished, possibly, from nonreal possessions: love, familial ties—wipes out the terrors of the past. At the same time, much like Ephraim Cabot, he keeps his sons in a tyrannically filial subjection, gaining identity thus as father and as man.

The mother has perhaps least force symbolically; she wanders about the edge of the action, energizing it, drawing love and attention, but asserting only an ancient identity: she was once beloved, wife, mother. She has no present, no future, only bare moments of contact with the immediate, and she seeks her final refuge in an escape into the past. But she does establish and integrate the familial structure.

The play, then, becomes the spectacle, the *agon*, of these four personal forces and identities, deriving from one central core of energy, acting upon one another, changing themselves as they change the others. It is the familial landscape, Freudian and Kafkaesque, with its corrosive intensities of unconscious and hidden and suppressed relationships, symbiotic or parasitic or magnetically repulsive, that becomes the universal setting: individuals alone and in relation to one another, living through one another, being human through being loved and loving, hated and hating, dependent and independent, parental and filial (all of these simultaneously, often). The background of *Long Day's Journey* is in the end that of Beckett's *Waiting for Godot*: the mortal situation, unplaced as to time, undelineated as to place.

Here are the Tyrones, once and for all defining themselves, fixing the moment of this achievement, and then cutting it under, not allowing it to remain clean and done. They sabotage themselves, alone and each other. Because they love one another, they exercise their love in hurting one another. But there is little blindness about this; only in utter sobriety do they deceive themselves, or try to deceive the others. As the dark closes in on them, the truth keeps emerging larger and larger, the huge lurking beast reveals itself.

"I meant it as a tribute to your love and tenderness," O'Neill wrote in dedicating the play to his wife—"your love and tenderness which gave me the faith in love that enabled me to face my dead at last and write this play—write it with deep pity and understanding and forgiveness for all the four haunted Tyrones."

Whatever the anguish at the source of *Long Day's Journey into Night*, the destination of the journey is finally the calm and peace of the acceptance that comes with soul-deep understanding. The conclusion of the play is infused with the wisdom of Oedipus at Colonus; of Lear sheltering the dying Cordelia and accepting life as it is, including death; of fathers and sons, of brothers, of human beings, reconciled to their mortal limitations but modestly, quietly, sadly celebrating these.

3

Mr. Eliot's Drama
His Jew and His Jazz Rhythms

Almost no serious critical attention has been paid to the portrait of the Jew in T. S. Eliot's early poetry or in his drama. This neglect is unfortunate, for the design of this portrait intertwines a number of motifs in the total work that have generally been considered discrete and unconnected. And a study of it is relevant to understanding Eliot's experiments in developing a dramatic style and tone. As Eliot's poetry influenced one generation, so his nearly neglected drama seems to be affecting another.

The Jew's basic meaning may be seen quickly in connection with one of the important and recurring themes in Eliot, man's relation to love and sexuality. "The extent to which Eliot's poetry is directly concerned with love," Delmore Schwartz wrote, "is matched only by the extent to which it is concerned with religious belief and the crisis of moral values. . . . Eliot's characters when they make love either suffer from what the psychoanalysts term 'psychic impotence,' or they make love so inadequately that the lady is left either hysterical or indifferent when the episode is over." Mr. Schwartz was writing about Eliot's early poems, but an unsuccessful marriage is at the heart of *The Family Reunion*, written in the thirties; and *The Cocktail Party*, of the late forties, is about "A man who finds himself incapable of loving / And a woman who finds that no man can love her."

But if Burbank is the impotent Englishman—or American—in need of a Baedeker to guide him through life, whose impotence, as his name suggests, may be the result of experiments in hybridization—if Burbank fails in a sexual competition, who then succeeds? The man with the Jewish name: Sir Ferdinand Klein. Eliot's attitude, at least at the time he wrote the poem, toward Sir Ferdinand, and supposedly toward all Jews endowed with incongruous titles who were displacing the members of his own caste sexually and otherwise, was bitterly derisive. "She entertains Sir Ferdinand," concludes one stanza. The pause, the hesitation, as the line turns, carries the contemptuous unwillingness to sound Sir Ferdinand's anticlimactic last name, "Klein," which is spit out as the first word of the next stanza. And the momentum of the rhythm suggests, in answer to the punctuation, that it was Klein "who clipped the lion's wings / And flea'd his rump and pared his claws."

All Jews and all characters with suggestively "Jewish" names appear in the poetry in unpleasant sexual situations. "Rachel née Rabinovitch" is a whore involved in some nasty conspiracy. "Pneumatic bliss" is promised by Grishkin. Eliot was uncomfortably aware of the great exodus from Russia and other lands of Eastern Europe to the West in the years immediately before the poem was written. "Swarming hordes," he called the people involved in it. Most of them, of course, were Jewish. At least two of the clients of Dusty and Doris's bordello in "Sweeney Agonistes" have Jewish names. And the "jew" in "Gerontion" "squats on the window sill," "spawned in some estaminet of Antwerp."

Eliot made other group distinctions based on sexual manners. Sweeney, who, unlike Burbank, was not a member of Mr. Eliot's social group, can function sexually, but in a purely automatic way, like the small house agent's clerk in *The Waste Land,* "one of the low" who "makes a welcome of indifference" in the typist with whom he has union. Sweeney, as he himself drearily points out, conceives of life as nothing but "birth, and copulation, and death, / That's all, that's all, that's all, that's all." "Love" in Sweeney's milieu is a matter of contraceptives, abortions, and sordidly listless seductions.

But while the sexual life of the low, as Eliot saw it, is mechanical, his Jews are lecherous (consider Bleistein's grotesque leering), voluptuous, violent. Eliot described them as primitive and bestial. Bleistein's "lustreless protrusive eye stares from the protozoic slime." "Rachel née Rabinovitch / Tears at the grapes with murderous paws." Jews are underneath the rats that are "underneath the piles." Grishkin has "a rank feline smell." In "Gerontion," the Jew "squats" on the window sill, simian (or toad) fashion; he was "spawned"; he is associated with the lascivious goat. Leslie A. Fiedler has suggestively described Eliot's depiction of the Jew "always in a low animal context" as "almost compulsive." By contrast, the animals that represent Eliot and his society are the "noble" ones like the lion and eagle, or, when he is satirical, a merely gigantic one, like the hippopotamus.

The Jew, then, stands in Eliot for the dark, the irrationally physical, the merely instinctive forces of emotion, animal emotion, the horror of succumbing to which pervades his early poetry. Conrad's Mr. Kurtz, it will be remembered, allowed himself to become the victim of just such a horror. So significant for Eliot was Kurtz's rise and fall in the heart of this darkness that he originally used the epigraph "Mistah Kurtz— he dead" for the epical *Waste Land.* The comment of Pound that it did not seem weighty enough for that poem caused Eliot to remove it and save it for "The Hollow Men." In view of the importance Eliot attached to Kurtz, is it significant that Kurtz's model in real life was named "Klein"? Eliot thought of these nonintellectual forces as the overwhelming danger to his civilization. Malcolm Cowley remarked that Eliot "defended the intellect as against the emotions, and the conscious mind as against the libido, the dark Freudian wish." Eliot's antisexuality and anti-Semitism, not really to be separated from one another, were part of his distaste for humanity in the mass.

The clearest dramatic presentation in Eliot of the conflict between the primitive unconscious and the carefully cultivated conscious occurs in *Sweeney Agonistes*, in which are merged the African and the Attic. Gilbert Murray, in the preface to his translation of *The Libation Bearers*, which was published a few years before *Sweeney Agonistes*, suggested the theme of Eliot's drama when he asked: "Where in all literature, except Aeschylus, could one find this union of primitive ghostliness with high intellectual passion? One hand seems to reach out to the African or Polynesian, while the other clasps that of Milton or Goethe." One of the epigraphs to *Sweeney Agonistes* is from Orestes' last speech in *The Libation Bearers*. It refers to the Erinyes, the punishing spirits. "You don't see them, you don't—but *I* see them: they are hunting me down, I must move on."

Who are the hunters? Who is being hunted? The Furies, to judge from Eliot's play, are the common people in general—here particularized as Sweeney, the prostitutes, the Jewish customers from America and their fallen English friends, and possibly Negroes: one character, Snow, appears as the traditional black-faced minstrel, "Bones"—and not only, as has been suggested, the Jews. I think it plain that it is Eliot who is being driven, and not Sweeney, as Stephen Spender be-

lieves. Why should Sweeney feel hunted by his con-
frères? Unless, of course, Sweeney represents an aspect
of Eliot.

The second quotation, which is from St. John of the
Cross, elucidates the first. It concerns mystical purgation. "Hence the soul cannot be possessed of the divine
union, until it has divested itself of the love of created
beings." Whether "love of" means "love for" or "love
belonging to," and whether Eliot is ridding himself of
his feeling for humanity or its feeling for him, it would
seem clear from the play that Eliot believes his own
cleansing requires the annihilation of any emotional
connection between him and mankind. *Sweeney Agonistes* may be read as ending in a mass orgiastic death,
not unlike the concluding sexual finale of Greek comedy.
The loathsome world has destroyed itself with sex.

Love in Eliot is always sexual; we rarely see any other
manifestation of it in his work, such as the filial or
platonic; toward sexual love, his attitude is either of re-
signed acceptance of its inhuman machinelike practice
or repugnance toward what he takes to be dissoluteness.
All of his creatures, one way or another, are contempt-
ible or pathetic in their sex habits, but a special con-
demnation seems to be reserved for the emotionally
vulgar Jews.

The prose gives substance to the anti-emotional bias
adumbrated in the poems. In 1927 Eliot approved of the
movement "toward a higher and clearer conception of
Reason, and a more severe and serene control of the
emotions by Reason." Some years later, he objected to
"prejudice and excessive emotion" as appropriate guides
for reacting to genocide. He equated romanticism with
"heresy." "Extreme emotionalism seems to me a symp-
tom of decadence," he said in commenting on Hardy.
"What is disastrous is that the writer should deliberately
give rein to his individuality." "Personality," for him,

can become "a thing of alarming importance." Eliot
opposed the self-indulgence of modern life with "discip-
line, inconvenience and discomfort" as the means to
his utopia. In rejecting liberalism, he says that it "tends
to release energy rather than accumulate it, to relax,
rather than to fortify."

In *After Strange Gods*, Eliot brought together the
literary and religious components of his opposition to
emotion. The most significant section of this work seems
to me to be the attack on D. H. Lawrence: "Lawrence
is for my purposes, an almost perfect example of the
heretic." F. R. Leavis, who early recognized the peculiar importance of Eliot's objections to Lawrence,
suggested that the polarity of the two men might be
found in their extreme positions on sex. Eliot's "attitudes with reference to sex," pointed out Leavis, "have
been, in prose and poetry, almost uniformly nega-
tive—attitudes of distaste, disgust, and rejection."
Lawrence, on the other hand, of course, always labored,
as he himself said, and as Mr. Leavis emphasized, "to
make the sex relation valid and precious, not shame-
ful." It is apt, of course, that Eliot, the perpetually self-
conscious and authoritarian Christian, should set up
Lawrence as his arch opponent, Lawrence with his concept of "blood consciousness," with his apotheosis of
the emotional, totally responsive man, with his rejection
of externally imposed rules for living. We may dismiss
Eliot's late modification of his position on Lawrence.
To quote Leavis again: "It perpetuates the misconcep-
tions, misrepresentations and misdirections that have
already, over so long a period, worked so much mis-
chief. Not only does Mr. Eliot make no recantation;
he shows himself to be still unemancipated from his
disabling prejudices."

It was in *After Strange Gods*, while defining heresy
and arguing for the necessity to art of a stable, orthodox

culture, that Eliot made the remarks most often quoted by polemicists—incompletely—to "prove" his anti-Semitism.

> The population should be homogeneous; where two or more cultures exist in the same place they are likely either to be fiercely self-conscious or both to become adulterate. What is still more important is unity of religious background; and reasons of race and religion combine to make any large number of free thinking Jews undesirable.

Eliot was opposed in this passage, as David Daiches has generally remarked, to "the pluralistic culture toward which Western civilization has been moving since the Renaissance." Eliot's philosophical objection to the mixing of cultures, of course, was the counterpart of his distaste for miscegenation.

It seems to me easy to argue against Eliot's insistence that a monolithic, intolerant *Christian* tradition is the sine qua non for a modern artist, but I cannot see how his position was "anti-Semitic" in any of the usual senses we give that term. Freethinking Jews happen to sabotage Eliot's utopia on two grounds: they have neither religion nor a tradition of any considerable length or body—as yet—nor, obviously, Christianity. Our argument with him should be waged, as Philip Rahv put it, "on wholly non-sectarian grounds, such as that the new religiosity is hostile to the best interests of the mind; that it tends to divide rather than unite humanity; and that it is historically vacuous and metaphysically permeated with a romantic nostalgia making it easy to evade the truly urgent problems of modern man."

But Mr. Eliot's religiosity cannot really be separated from any of his other activities; his practice of his religion, his attempts to understand it in relation to himself and the world, as in perhaps no artist since Dante, were intimately mingled with his perpetually probing assaults on poetry, morals, and literary values. Edmund Wilson made just this point. "We recognize throughout *The Waste Land* the peculiar conflicts of the Puritan turned artist: the horror of vulgarity and the shy sympathy with the common life, the ascetic shrinking from sexual experience and the distress at the drying up of the springs of sexual emotion, with the straining after a religious emotion which may be made to take its place."

"Straining," with its suggestion of the artificial, may be the key word in understanding the man. Eliot's progress from St. Louis, his merely physical birthplace, a city of ambiguous tradition, neither southern nor northern; through New England, the home of his immediate forebears, but still an uncertain refuge for him; and finally to his spiritual haven and his ancient birthplace, England—this northeasterly migration homeward, exactly reversing the course of the rugged, restless, earlier Puritans, this rolling up to its source of the carpet of his ancestral experience, was a controlled demonstration of an attitude. Eliot always sought just the right tone in expression; his famous recantations, for example, whatever we may think about their content, indicated his restless dissatisfaction with the less than permanently applicable. He seemed always to have known the usefulness of assuming poses in the study of his relationship to the world.

Eliot came to England prepared to drape about himself the mantle of what he took to be the best aristocratic British tradition: Conservatism, royalism, Anglicanism, and whatever else happened to go along with these. He may have been especially eager in those days, amid the alien corn, to show an acceptance of everything else—the minor attitudes, the unimportant snobberies—since his claim to assuming the major orthodoxies was specious. Roots do thin out at some distance to hairlike fineness. It was during these years that he dabbled with fascism, an aristocratic pastime of the moment. And it is exclusively in the poems published in the twenties that the descriptions of ugly Jews appear.

When Eliot was writing these poems, and for some years before, philo-Semitism, a product of Victorian sentimentalism and liberalism and the British reaction against the Dreyfus affair, filled the air. Israel Zangwill during these years was at the height of his fame; Eliot was still rather unknown. Possibly Eliot reacted against the prevalent feeling toward Jews precisely because of its widespread nature and adopted (may even have helped to revive) the more ancient one, the more "orthodox" one of sinister hostility. Eliot's Jew is certainly even more sensualist than merchant or cosmopolite, although sexual sophistication is a component of cosmopolitanism. In addition, the myth of the Jew as sexual villain could satisfy Eliot in relation to his own sexual disenchantment. And the financial caricature (the Jew in furs and Sir Alfred Mond wrapped in a five-percent bond) may have had meaning in connection with his unhappy early job as bank clerk.

But most important, perhaps, the Jew served Eliot in his straining to belong. European anti-Semitism in broadest terms—the irrational objections to the Jew's new wealth and ostentation and the possibly more rational ones on the grounds of his liberalism and humanism, for Jews undeniably were in the forefront of scientific and social enlightenment and political revolution—this all-inclusive anti-Semitism had a tradition among the occupants of that stratum of European society in which Eliot was seeking a perch. It has been argued with some cogency that Eliot used the portrait of the Jew as a symbol of the decline of the modern world, of the decline of the Jews themselves. But it requires a certain point of view toward the world to see it only in ruins, to turn so totally from humanity in disgust and defeat, to see Jews exclusively as fallen figures rather than, at least in part, as among the leaders of a new contemporary humanism, which, indeed, was preparing the way for the emergence of artists like Eliot himself.

Briefly, this fashionable anti-Semitism, as Hannah Arendt among others has pointed out, is a thoroughly modern thing, developed as a device, sometimes minor, sometimes of chief utility, frequently unconscious, in the technique of undermining democracy. In literature it expressed itself in an utter despair of modern life. Consider Graham Greene, Céline, Pound, Roy Campbell. Eliot's espousals of fascism, however amorphous and qualified, his "anti-Semitism," or whatever we may consider it, his glorification of authority, were the complementary positive expressions of his morbid denial of individualism and his denigration of emotion.

The purity of Eliot's withdrawal from the mob, however, was always adulterated by a longing to mix with it. Edmund Wilson described Eliot's simultaneous revulsion from and attraction by vulgarity. While Eliot condemned Sweeney, he also, in his own way, envied him. The championing of Kipling offers a neat demonstration of this ambivalence. Lionel Trilling in his review of Eliot's edition of Kipling's poems made much of this odd association of highbrow and lowbrow.

Mr. Eliot speaks of "the fascination of exploring a mind so different from my own," and certainly the difference between the two minds is the quietly dramatic point of his elaborate public appearance with Kipling. But we are tempted—and perhaps Mr. Eliot wishes us to be tempted—to question the difference and look for the similarity. And poetically the affinity

is not so impossible as it seems. . . . It is significant
that among the dominant themes of both Kipling and
Eliot is the fear of a nameless psychological horror
and despair. Politically they share the headlong
and angry reliance on administration and authority.
They have the same sense of being beset and betrayed
by the ignoble mob; Kipling invented and elaborated
the figure of the "Pict," the dark, little, hating man
who in other guises plays so important a part in Mr.
Eliot's poetry, who stimulates in both the pathos of
xenophobia, one manifestation of which is an open
and reasoned anti-Semitism.

Of course, while the Jew was the most prominent figure
in Eliot's gallery of outsiders, we should not forget,
among other creatures, the obsequious Hakagawa of
"Gerontion" or the unshaved, Levantine, homosexual
Mr. Eugenides of *The Waste Land.* That "sense of being beset and betrayed by the ignoble mob" was just
that general incapacity of Eliot to immerse himself—
without writing the script and casting the characters—
in humanity, and in life.

At this point, it would appear, Eliot's relation to Lawrence becomes fully significant, not least perhaps because Lawrence's Jewish stereotype was that of an intellectual. The distinctions between the two are crucial.
Lawrence affirmed the glory of life: his sexuality was a
celebration of human living. *The Waste Land,* with its
climax of resignation and acceptance ("The Peace that
passeth understanding") was possibly as much a con-
tented memorial hymn as a lament over the sterility of
modern civilization. The sadness in Eliot has a strangely
smug satisfaction about it. While Lawrence often felt
dubious about mankind and had to construct utopias to
save it, he was always hopeful and positive; his energy
was outgoing, hopefully directed, and never constric-

tive. His sadness expressed itself in passion and anger, not in submission. In the character of their opposition, our time, as Leavis said, "may fairly be called the age of D. H. Lawrence and T. S. Eliot."

Eliot expressed himself in the thirties and forties as aggrieved that his representation of the Jew should have been considered "anti-Semitic." Perhaps his Jew should be taken as a purely dramatic creation, and his tone toward him merely as an affectation. Yet all this cannot be dismissed. Although Eliot in his lifetime put on different demeanors for different reasons, such as momentary needs of the personality or changes in history, there did exist an unchangeable visage beneath, difficult to make out in its complete natural form, but discernible in some of the lineaments it forced through the various masks. A study of the essential Eliot shows the almost casual, surely momentary nature of his portraits of Jews. But it reveals also that for many years he was incapable of sympathy, not alone with Jews, but with humanity at large. This failure of feeling, of comfortable and unhedged identification, he seems to have recognized and to have been dealing with in his austere but mellow late work. There is a kind of rueful irony in the acceptance into the family by marriage of B. Kaghan, another man with a Jewish name, whose vulgarity is tempered by his engaging vitality and the promise, even, to assume a new gentility.

Yet it is an early, purportedly unfinished dramatic work that best adumbrates Eliot's future. In its mixing of drunken conversation, pessimistic philosophy, gruesome anecdotes, jazz rhythms, minstrel show badinage, brassy vaudeville lyrics, despicable persons (prostitutes, vulgar Americans, and an accessory to murder), mindless repetitions, *Sweeney Agonistes* achieves a sometimes surrealistic, nightmarish quality anticipating much later works like Michael McClure's *The Beard*.

In some ways, *Sweeney Agonistes* bears a relation both to "Kubla Khan" and "Christabel," two other famous fragments. "Christabel," like *Sweeney Agonistes*, was a poem written in an experimental meter. But the kinship is much stronger, I think, with "Kubla Khan." With little difficulty, "Kubla Khan" can be read as a poem complete in itself: an expression of guilt as a result of artistic creation; Coleridge himself is the sorcerer with the flashing eyes, the floating hair, having just created a poem. Similarly, *Sweeney Agonistes* seems to be an entity. After fulfilling the "instructions" of the prefaced quotations, what else was there to say? And, indeed, after using jazz rhythms, the language of the low, to destroy the low, there was no other use for jazz rhythms, and Eliot never returned to them for his later poetry. In spite of Eliot's later inclusion of *Sweeney Agonistes* under "Unfinished Poems," I think we may read it as a complete unit that fulfills its author's intentions.

In his late work Eliot abandoned jazz rhythms for rather obvious reasons: jazz rhythms were hardly appropriate to philosophical and religious matter. But his experiments in prosody, his delight in the metrics of W. S. Gilbert and Kipling, indicated an awareness and a demonstration of the possibilities in creating a poetry for a wide audience. "The dependence of verse upon speech," Eliot remarked, "is much more direct in dramatic poetry than in any other." The blank verse of Shakespeare bore a derivative relationship to Elizabethan speech, as Shaw insisted. "No poetry," Eliot also said, "of course, is ever exactly the same speech that the poet talks and hears: but it has to be in such a relation to the speech of his time that the listener or reader can say 'that is how I should talk if I could talk poetry.' This is the reason why the best contemporary poetry can give us a feeling of excitement and a sense of fulfillment different from any sentiment aroused by even very much greater poetry of a past age."

Any verse drama in any period has to be built on a similar relationship in order to achieve popularity. Eliot's *Sweeney Agonistes* and his book of children's verses would seem to indicate that any present-day poetic drama to reach wide audiences and retain a genuine poetic quality would have to be written in meters and idioms that can catch and hold—for whatever reasons—the attention of everyone: "We have still a good way to go in the invention of a verse medium for the theatre," Eliot said, "a medium in which we shall be able to hear the speech of contemporary human beings, in which dramatic characters can express the purest poetry without high-falutin and in which they can convey the most commonplace message without absurdity."

It is interesting that in his late comments on verse-drama, in his lecture on "Poetry and Drama" at Harvard in 1950, for example, Eliot added almost nothing new to his earlier examinations. There is one hint, however, which would suggest the banishment of jazz rhythms in future experiments for a reason of technique. "We can never emulate music," he said, "because to arrive at the condition of music would be the annihilation of poetry, and especially of dramatic poetry." But has not exactly this "annihilation" already taken place —in addition to the other annihilation suggested—in *Sweeney Agonistes*? It is an early instance of Western nondrama. In Eliot, as in all great artists, style and content are ultimately one, and the experiments of one age become the idioms of a later one.

4

The Jewishness of Arthur Miller
His Family Epic

Arthur Miller was born in 1915. His career, more closely perhaps than that of any other popularly successful writer, closely followed a scenario for the mid-century intellectual hero: Jewish, born and raised in New York, University of Michigan during the Depression, commitment to radical causes, first novel a succès d'estime, Pulitzer Prize for playwriting (1949), marriage to a screen goddess, subsequent divorce, prophet and spokesman for liberal causes. Miller came to maturity through the agonies of the Depression and the political turmoils of the forties, when guilt was in the air: "capitalists" accused of responsibility for the economic condition; "imperialists" of responsibility for the deteriorated international situation; "intellectuals" of indifference to the "masses" and to the coming revolution.

All of Miller's plays deal with some aspect of guilt, but in four, particularly, he sets the matter in the specific context of a family with two sons: *All My Sons* (1947), *Death of a Salesman* (1949), *After the Fall* (1964), and *The Price* (1968). We may read these four plays as a kind of Galsworthian family tetralogy, an integrated saga in which there is a thematic progression. The plays may be read, indeed, as works about the same family considered under changing circumstances and from different perspectives. The development from first play to fourth play provides a record of some of the changing values of American middle-class family life during the period in which they were written.

All My Sons is simple in conception and execution. The earliest of his plays, it is also the most "well-made" in the Scribean sense, plainest and most schematic. The emphasis is heavy-handedly social. Joe Keller, while building his business for his two sons, is so caught up by what he refers to as the "dog-eat-dog" character of capitalistic society that he neglects his responsibility toward all the sons of this world, that is, to all society. During World War II, in order to fulfill a contract deadline, he allows to be sent out of his plant defective parts for airplanes. The airplanes crash, killing their occupants. Keller kills himself.

Keller's guilt is narrow and personal, limited to himself, arising from that one crime committed against society. His own corruption has not extended to his family. The sons are extravagant idealists unlike their father, an uncomplicated materialist. One son kills himself on learning of his father's crime. The other has talked a life of such high-minded devotion to ideals that he becomes offensive to a neighbor, the practical wife of the physician next door who dreams of going off to starve in a laboratory while fighting an epidemic. The two boys are guilty of nothing, not even of being their father's sons. Keller's wife sustains the fantasy that her son is not dead, in order to continue supporting and loving her husband.

While *Death of a Salesman* may be read as no less social than *All My Sons,* its focus has become wider. Biff and Happy are much more their father's sons. Willy Loman has made them what they are. Willy's own guilt is familial, related not only to his wife and sons and affecting them, but entangled also with his own brother. Unlike Joe Keller, who enjoys only a moment of introspection and insight before he kills himself, Willy spends much of the time before he kills himself oppressed by his guilt and inadequacy. Keller, of course, knew plainly enough what he was guilty of since he committed a single, clear-cut criminal act that is asserted to have had awful consequences. Willy Loman never finds out what his "guilt" is, social or personal. Clearly, that guilt has something to do with his own inadequacy as man and father. About the only self-understanding he achieves is his poignant comment that he has always felt "temporary."

The consequences of Keller's social crime are alluded to, not dramatically presented or sustained. We are told of the deaths of the pilots; we hear the shot ending Keller's life. Except for his wife's defiantly sustained fantasy that their son is still alive, no other effect of Keller's crime is observable in the text of the play. All significant action involving Keller has already taken place. By contrast, the consequences of Willy Loman's guilt are presented every moment. His punishment does not simply climax the play, as Keller's suicide in *All My Sons* climaxes that play. Willy's suicide simply climaxes his punishment. His "crime," whatever it is, and the punishment are the play. Willy alternates between the euphoria of a self-deceiving confidence and the agony of disappointment throughout; the euphoria and the agony combine to produce his torture.

If guilt has roots, if there is a dynamics to guilt that acquires its impetus in the past, then Keller is nearly innocent. He certainly cannot be charged with making his sons crass. We might even give him his due for making them so decent. It was indeed his partner, as Keller tells us, who had a history of blaming others for his own errors. So strong is that history, the partner's own children believe that their father was actually guilty of the original crime. Joe Keller has never had second thoughts about his way of life. His suicide is nearly gratuitous, for he might have continued his bluff of innocence—if it was bluff. In *Death of a Salesman*, guilt is made organic; it is integrated with everything a man thinks, feels, does, becomes. Willy's guilt, however, is never defined, never given an origin or examined in its development, and never anatomized.

The sustained self-doubt of Willy Loman, the father, is shifted in *After the Fall* to Quentin, the son. Willy's one poignant question to Bernard, "What—what's the secret?" becomes a whole text. (Willy himself is reincarnated in *After the Fall* in the person and life of Quentin's father, a reincarnation emphasized in the original New York production by the resemblance of the actor playing the role to Lee J. Cobb, the original Willy Loman.) Quentin is a mingling of Biff and of Bernard in *Death of a Salesman*; he is a lawyer (who is even scheduled to appear, like Bernard, before the Supreme Court), one of whose problems seems to be that he wants to be well-liked by everyone.

But Quentin marks an advance over Willy. He comes a generation later. He has the resources of enlightened, intellectual self-investigation to help him define himself and to determine the sources and character of his guilt. Where Marx is called on to account for Keller, Freud is enlisted in behalf of Quentin. (In *Death of a Salesman*, Marx collaborates with Freud, Marx arranging the business world, Freud the private one. This may account for the mixture of causes producing various disasters. Willy's job as a salesman gets crushed in the relentless operations of capitalism; Biff's incapacity to achieve maturity is, in good measure, the result of a classically simple Oedipal shock, finding his father unfaithful to his mother.) One consequence of Quentin's massive, monumental, sophisticated confessional is that he seems very nearly to absolve himself of any guilt at all, certainly of any personal guilt.

After the Fall insists on the mortality of man, on his natural, postlapsarian, general, eternal culpability. Quentin is not only Adam, uxoriously weak and self-abasing; he is in sudden brief flashes even Christ. And no wonder. His extraordinary, solipsistic monologue, the structure of the play, evokes the existence of all other characters. Their presence on the stage only in relation to himself, coming back again and again, sometimes freezing to hold a particularly traumatic or charged moment, results in a megalomanic enlargement of self. Quentin goes from first and representative man to divine man. Guilt is not merely forgiven him but is made the occasion for revelation and apotheosis.

After the Fall is extravagant in its ambition to pull together the strands of social, familial, and personal guilt which appear in the earlier plays. Guilt becomes a fashioned baroque monster here, and it is only an ancient, private, singlehanded, chivalric boldness that can seek it out and destroy it. Miller has moved from the time-limited, social, anecdotal atmosphere of *All My Sons* to the universal, heroic, sagalike one of *After the Fall*.

Miller's emphasis in these three plays has been on the favored (or surviving, or eldest) son of the family. In *All My Sons*, society is determined by material values alone; this is the skeletally simple Marxist structure. In *Death of a Salesman*, it is not the society alone which is so important; it is the honesty of one's relations to that society which at least affects character and deed. Miller has enlarged his sense of society in *Death of a Salesman* to include man in something of his mystery and whimsicality. In *After the Fall*, he has very nearly excluded from his microscopic focus every territory except the interior personal one. But man must function in context. For all his meanderings and maunderings through the spaces of mind and memory, Quentin must return, if he returns at all, to the mundane and social. This is all mortal man can be fit for. Even Adam had to enter the world. The exaggerated if simple idealism of Chris Keller as a way of coping, Willy Loman's pathetic fumbling, are replaced by Quentin's enormously complex, self-forgiving pragmatism.

Quentin's candor in his confessional apologia appears absolute, that is, he leaves nothing out; he blocks nowhere. Yet he repeatedly seems to insist on offering excessively ugly, awful, or simply distasteful details so as not to seem to be sparing himself about possibly less awful ones. (He'd rather have his wife call him a fairy than a Jew.) On such a busy canvas, an area of utter whiteness must stand out, especially if our eye is directed to it by the thrusts and movements surrounding it.

What is Quentin's ethnic identification?

The ethnic anonymity of these plays is striking, if only by contrast with the plays of Odets and O'Neill, whose Jewish and Irish Catholic families in *Awake and Sing* and in *Long Day's Journey into Night* are so plainly identified for us. In both these plays, it is the ethnic particularity that provides the operative rationale for much of the dynamics of motivation and action. In Miller, mysteries arise because we simply do not know where the characters come from, what their habits are, their ambitions, their values.

It is difficult to find ethnic clues in Miller. It is perhaps simple to account for this difficulty in *All My Sons*, for the play has a general two-dimensionality in plot and character. It purports to be "universally" social. But even here, at least one striking moment occurs to suggest, however thinly, the world of the Jewish mother. The son of Keller's imprisoned partner appears on the scene to keep his sister from marrying Keller's surviving son. Mrs. Keller, pretending obliviousness of her husband's machinations, fawns over the partner's son with a familiar, Jewish mother's concern. "Look at him. . . . He looks like a ghost. . . . Sit down. I'll make you a sandwich."

Willy Loman's Jewishness is more critical. How is it that Willy, living in a Brooklyn neighborhood where other sons are named Bernard and are encouraged by their parents to be superior in scholarship and to become lawyers, calls his sons Biff and Happy and wants them to be athletic heroes? Why is it that Willy lusts after Dale Carnegie, Joe DiMaggio signs of American success, a Rotarian "popularity" independent of achievement, an athletic prowess that turns one for a period into a folk hero? Willy seems devoted to becoming "American," in obvious and large ways, as well as in small and perhaps mysterious ways. He wants the glamorous success that comes from adventurous exploring; he worships Uncle Ben who appears in the play only in passage from one exotic and profitable enterprise to another. But he also enjoys the mindless and irresponsible pleasures of carpentry, of working with his hands, the ineffable delights of the artisan.

Perhaps nothing is so revealing in exposing Willy's wish to be anything but himself, which, in any case, he never has clearly defined, as the intensity of his fury with Charlie. Charlie is self-acceptingly Jewish, and his needling questions to Willy, even his gestures of charity, pierce through Willy's insulation, for these are always forcing Willy to face himself.

Not the least of Willy's failures is that his sons, no lawyers, no athletic heroes, no well-liked Rotarians, no businessmen, have become drifting cowhands in the West, occasional jailbirds, drunkards, and whoremasters. Biff and Happy achieve one form of the peculiarly Jewish vision, the peculiarly fearful image, of the American as bum. Not even Willy can kid himself about this sort of assimilationism. (Henry Popkin in an essay in *Commentary* suggested that the "misfits" in Miller's

movie script with that name were Biff and Happy trans-
planted to the world of Reno and rodeos.)

One has to ask what meaning there may be in the
sequence, not just the details, of the events of Quentin's
life. Quentin rejects his father's wish for him to go into
the family business (reminding us of Chris Keller), becomes a lawyer who first defends and then rejects an old
friend and teacher called before a Congressional com-
mittee investigating Communism, divorces his first
wife to marry a singer who becomes enormously popular, and finally commits himself to a relationship with
a non-Jewish German woman, whose relatives were
Nazis, and with whom he visits a former concentration
camp. He expresses guilt for abandoning his father, his
wife, his family, his friend and teacher, the victims of
the concentration camps (although this is confused and
mysterious). The litany prepares us (and him) for his
marriage to the German girl.

We know how much the critics have made of the
autobiographical parallels between Quentin and Miller;
but most of them were talking about obvious and, in
large measure, indifferent details. I think the point to
be made is how remarkably unautobiographical the play
tries to be. Quentin's very name suggest the wish to leap
away from the thinginess of his life (and, paradoxically,
suggests it, for he comes from a time when the fashions
in Jewish child-naming tended toward the "Anglo-
Saxon" sounding names); yet he never comes close in
his outpouring to his psychoanalyst (?), confessor (?),
public (?), himself (?) to identifying with name and
number what it is he is impelling himself away from.

Jewish life in America may still not have gone far
enough even in 1964 to keep one from using his Jewishness, both defensively and aggressively (the incompetent
who complains that his fate is the result only of anti-
Semitism), and then pretend not to be using it. This is

still the liberalism of the thirties, Miller's crucible, which on the one hand could argue that Jews and Negroes should not be discriminated against, and, on the other, that there are no Jews, no Negroes, only undifferentiated Americans.

The autobiographical import of *After the Fall*, then, may be found in the very absence of truly significant autobiographical matter. The mea culpa rings hollow. (The presentation of the hero as a famous lawyer, delighted by the literary effectiveness of his briefs, is so transparent a masking, and so unpersuasive dramatically, that it almost appears as if Miller wanted to make sure that no one could seriously mistake the hero's identity.)

If Quentin is *not* Jewish, how in the world did he get mixed up in all that Jewish history, with all those Jewish types: his first wife, whose stolid, self-righteous, shallow, self-taught intellectuality is as noisomely Jewish as a tenement hall on the East Side before supper; his father is depicted as nothing less than the Yiddisher King Lear, betrayed by his son, and the actor plays the role properly as Maurice Schwartz might have, on Second Avenue, with drawn out, self-pitying tantrums; his Americanized mother, properly West-End-Avenue-ish, with no Yiddish accent or intonation, is instinctively dedicated to emasculating the men in the family, like Bessie Berger in *Awake and Sing*; his former teacher behaves and sounds like one of the professors in the New York City colleges, most of them Jewish, discharged in the thirties for being members of the Party; the colleague he betrays, shrugging, arm-waving, and playing with language, is a stereotype of the New York Jewish "professional." That awful squirming and threshing about, even the ticlike shoulder shrugs, eyebrow raising, head tilting, hand-sawing, and thigh slapping, that Quentin on stage uses may mark the sheer physical efforts at extrication from his past, but if so all these gestures commit and root him to his origins. Jason Robards, the actor, as Quentin looked like a desperate Talmudist trying to prove by Talmudic gesturing, rhetorical self-questioning, and attempts at *chochma* that he was not a Talmudist. Robards has been quoted as saying that Kazan did not "direct" him; if true, his performance was a masterpiece of reading the text right: no other activity would have been so revealing of the *essential* meaning of Quentin's journey into himself.

Miller's three plays reflect a later and much changed phase of the Jewish experience in America than that recorded by Odets. Odets's Jews were still poor, enmired in the economic depression of the thirties, their speech still carrying overtones of Yiddish, still seeking self-definition and social place. Miller's are petits bourgeois, first generation professional, middle class and upper middle class, well on the way to an assimilation in the total culture, however occasionally uncomfortable.

What is missing in Miller is an accounting for that discomfort. It seems inadequate to say that Willy Loman went wrong because he took seriously hollow values. Why did he take them so? It is certainly inadequate to explain Quentin's incessant doubting of himself, because of what he takes to be the history of his rejections by persons close to him, with a simple Freudian mechanism, as the play tries to do. Quentin's "problem" no doubt must include in its genesis his parents' assault on his child's consciousness, their betrayal of his trust when they go on a weekend holiday, but his problem clearly also transcends that assault. One does not inevitably develop a nearly Christlike assumption of responsibility simply as a result of feeling rejected on one occasion when very young. In short, we miss the objective correlative for the excessiveness of emotion and behavior in Quentin.

Robert Warshow in his essays on *Death of a Salesman* and *The Crucible* refers to Miller's impulse toward abstracting and universalizing experience in order to achieve a generalized, large statement. In the process, Miller overlooks, adulterates, masks, or diminishes the particular. The ambition to make of a Willy Loman and of a Quentin a modern Everyman is worthy, but first each must be a someone. The progress from the external, flat surfaces of *All My Sons* to the endlessly rolling, cavernous, enclosed landscape of *After the Fall* marks, I think, Miller's effort to move into the interiors of experience. Simply, Miller has progressed *dramatically*. His work may still be filled with implausibilities, inconsistencies, sheer theatrical mistakes (that sister in *After the Fall* who never appears; the repeated cuts made in the text to shorten the performing time, which subtract nothing from the impact), but in *After the Fall*, he has tried at least to write from the inside out about almost recognizable persons facing almost recognizable realities. There is a minimum of "idea" imposed on the play, a maximum (which is, of course, too much) of passion.

More importantly, the self-delusion about their Jewishness of his heroes even seems to have been penetrated by Quentin's relentless honesty. Flail about long and hard enough in your memory and in your passion, and you're bound to cut through any padding of self-protection: it is difficult to believe that *Incident at Vichy*, the play that immediately followed *After the Fall*, in which a Gentile aristocrat sacrifices himself for a Jewish psychoanalyst, is not rooted somewhere in those misty, unfulfilled concentration-camp images of *After the Fall*. It is a kind of footnote to it.

Philip Rahv was outraged by the sacrificial dénouement of *Incident at Vichy*: "This Myshkin-like act of self-sacrifice seems to me to belie the entire portentous

dialectic of guilt, responsibility, the horror of Nazism
. . . which Miller develops throughout the entire production. It is a melodramatic contrivance pure and
simple, a sheer *coup de théâtre*." True, true, but how
human; how much the playwright wishes such a climax
and fulfills his fantasy needs, as in *After the Fall*. And
the point is that dramatically it works; it generates
enough plausibility to seem, at least dramatically, valid,
which is to say true for that moment. "It may give the
audience a lift," Rahv wrote, "but it drops the play's
intellectual baggage with a thud."

This, of course, has been Miller's strength and weak-
ness from the beginning, as it has been of other American playwrights, O'Neill's for example: the intellectual
content is often so far inferior to the dramatic achievement although the intellectual reach may be farther.
All My Sons, of course, is intellectually hackneyed
and barely has a dramatic substance to warrant taking
it seriously at all; it is a curiosity in the usual literary-
critical study of the work of a major writer. But it does
establish the family setting that is to preoccupy Miller
significantly for a period. *Death of a Salesman*, still the
most aesthetically successful of Miller's works, achieves
its power because the intellectuality becomes so deeply
buried under the dramatic texture. Challenge the text,
doubt it, deride the characters and their motivation, the
text remains to move one validly. But it is still program-
matic, written to sustain a thesis, and the only direction in which it could lead was to another porten-
tously "intellectual" work, *The Crucible*, which has had
to wait for the dissipation of the Joe McCarthyite vap-
ors to be read as a dramatic work mainly, not as a dis-
guised pamphlet. (It is remarkable how the familial
core of the play has a power, in and of itself, separate
from the thematic intent.)

In *The Price*, Miller takes up the sort of question that

comes after the satisfaction of survival and with the awareness of arrival and affluence: has the game been worth the candle? As in the earlier family plays, the two sons were in conflict with their father while he was alive, in different ways, and remain after his death in some significant conflict with one another. The play marks an advance as a family study in that the older son has achieved a measure of reconciliation with himself and with reality: after suffering a "breakdown," the word he uses, and going through a divorce, he announces that he has washed himself of "guilt." He is ambivalent about money and success, shrewdly knowledgeable in how to achieve either, but also, he says, quite ready to brush them aside. He has made a lifetime practice of moral compromise, a capacity not available to his more simpleminded brother. The difference in intellectual complexity between the two is heavily emphasized by their vastly different vocations: the older brother is a successful surgeon and medical businessman while the younger is a police sergeant on the New York force, ready to retire.

Throughout the play, the older brother emphasizes the point that he alone is responsible for ensuring his college career and subsequent success. He was cavalier about his responsibilities toward his father, who failed in business and thereafter vegetated, while his policeman brother felt it his personal responsibility to support the old man even at the expense of giving up college for himself. At a climactic moment, the older brother reveals that their father had always had enough money to have made it unnecessary for the younger brother to sacrifice his education.

The problem posed, then, is not unlike some of the problems raised in earlier plays: is the older brother's decision to pursue his college career really a morally ambiguous one, or is it simply based on information—

that the father can well support himself—not so clearly
available to his younger brother? Is the younger brother's fate the result of a large social force, like the economic depression of the thirties, *exclusively*, or is it as
much the result of the father's selfishness, the brother's
secretiveness, and his own hesitation to commit himself
to a long-range goal at some immediate risk? The contrivance implicit in the revelation is too much like the
mechanical device of an O. Henry or Guy de Maupassant
noble sacrifice carried through in ignorance of some essential piece of information. Can one's fate indeed be
critically changed by but one variable?

The Jewish emphasis in the play is intriguing. Interestingly, the family is not Jewish; it is, indeed, explicitly non-Jewish and aware of this. But the Jewishness in the play is omnipresent in the emphasis, for
example, on the intrinsic value of a college education as
though this alone is a treasure to be displayed: one
thinks of Miller's touching expression of gratitude, in his
essay about the University of Michigan, to the officials
for merely allowing him to go there. But it is the Jewishness of the ancient, shrewd furniture appraiser, who
comes to set the price on the household goods, that
dominates the play. The appraiser's role is so strong, so
expansively conceived and written, that he dominates
every scene. He is a kind of ghost, like that of Hamlet's
father, supervising and remarking on the activities of his
offspring. He comments on the exchanges between the
bickering brothers, emerging as the wryly wise choral
kibitzer so common to American Jewish family life. He
is also a more finished portrait of the shadowy Uncle
Ben, the successful adventurer who slips into and out
of scenes in *Salesman*. Almost like Tiresias, he has lived
through and suffered almost every human possibility.
But his main importance is as a philosophical, rabbini-
cal commentator on the point, the worth, the ends, the
values of life itself.

The issue of the price of the furniture becomes enlarged to include the price of any transaction, of any bargain that is struck in the world, of any memory or other possession or attainment that we may have gathered and cherished. Repeated variations are rung on the concept of price: what price does one pay for a happy marriage? For a successful career? To fulfill ambition? For breaking off family ties? For filial sacrifice? For civil service security? What price, even, do we pay for the very suit of clothes that covers our exteriors? Nothing is bought, nothing is bargained for, nothing is received without an appropriate payment. We get no bargains; we get nothing for nothing; sometimes indeed, we get nothing for a great deal.

The preoccupation among the educated, liberal, intellectually ambitious middle class with a "best buy," a formulation fixed in our time by Consumers Union, reflects that need to make a little go a long way, a need of a financially squeezed community. The obsession with "price," with "bargain," we need hardly emphasize, is a familiar enough Jewish phenomenon, the result of a socially and economically hostile environment: it becomes a means of coping and, in some extreme situations, of actual survival. But an obsession of this sort, not exposed to examination and modulation, can lead to sickness, become sickness itself, can become as malignant in a purely American way as Mrs. Craig's cold dedication to things, in George Kelly's play, or Mrs. Gereth's worship of beautiful property, in Henry James's *Spoils of Poynton*.

Although a "surgeon" and a "policeman" may be much like a "salesman" in allegorical import, Miller does seem to be advancing toward a more open confrontation with the raw material from which he has fashioned these family works. At the same time, he has not abandoned his concern with "symbol" and the making of large philosophical statements, an impulse clearly reflected in his titles and in the underlying concerns these titles suggest: *All My Sons, Death of a Salesman, After the Fall, The Price,* each implying a dimension beyond the immediate and concrete.

Miller in *The Price* is still trying to understand the phenomenological particularity of contemporary American life through some large-focusing generalization. In his concern for such structuring, the small moment encapsulating a large "idea," he also suggests the point of the old-fashioned concern with the well-made play: there *is* order in the universe, and it can be represented in a careful control of event on stage. The good-natured whimsicality of the old furniture appraiser is divine in its patient benignity, in its gratuitousness, in its radiating and impersonal benevolence. There may be a price exacted for all bargains in this world, but the person setting this price is genial, amiable, kindly, forgiving, if ultimately hard-nosed about true worth. God is not only omniscient, knowing both the price of everything and its true value as well, and omnipotent, able to exact the right price finally in all situations, but, lest we tend to lacerate ourselves too mercilessly for our greed or stupidity, benevolent. We need, then, not be sensitive about being shortchanged: we will get the right price in the end. This meliorism accords with the American Jewish experience in its most obvious and in its coarsest aspects, and perhaps it is still too early to expect to find any subtler truths recorded in popular drama. At least Miller has gone beyond Eliot in demythicizing the Jew.

5

Musical Drama and the American Liberal Impulse

Modern musical theatre in America has been thoroughly surveyed. Perhaps no other single subject in the American theatre has been the object of so much attention: individual composers have had volumes devoted to their work; pictorial histories abound; performances are reproduced on records which sell in the hundreds of thousands; television documentaries have surveyed the scene; the movies cover the lives of musical comedy figures in the company of other American popular heroes. Some critics and theatrical historians have described American musical drama as one of the few authentically American contributions to the theatre. Some have deplored the fact that the expense of production makes it impossible for musical comedy to break into very new territory.

American musical theatre has assumed many shapes and taken many turns. Even if we exclude the minstrel show, vaudeville, burlesque, the *Ziegfeld Follies*, White's *Scandals*, Radio City Music Hall productions, and other forms of sheer musical and dance spectacle for which no significant script may be discerned, we still confront an enormous range of quality and intention. In any one season, for example, we may find ourselves with a work that evokes, however thinly, the spirit of Bertolt Brecht, as in *Cabaret*, side by side with another that simply exploits the nightclub landscape of Las Vegas in order to justify the appearance of a pair of stars and the presentation of loosely strung together musical numbers, as in *Golden Rainbow*.

As with other forms of popular entertainment not derived from a text, most musical comedies have simply vanished from memory, remaining only part of some historical record, undistinguished as to content and ambition. However, the significant musical works incorporating ideas have not only been influential in determining the direction of the form generally but have often recorded trends in the theatre at large and have in turn affected that theatre. While Broadway operators kept contriving ways of enlarging and making more spectacular various sorts of musical comedy, for example, including one that assumed the proportion very nearly of a circus, Billy Rose's *Jumbo*, off-Broadway enterprises were using music satirically for social comment, much like the nonmusical Broadway theatre.

Satirical commentary on social and political affairs is, of course, not original in the American theatre. Gilbert and Sullivan achieved their fame with such commentary, the immediate force of which may have been diminished after the contemporary event, but which still spices, more and more mildly as the years go on, the Gilbert and Sullivan repertory. Well-established college entertainments, like those at Columbia, Harvard, and Princeton, and the annual National Press Club production in Washington, are famous for their use of the immediate passing scene as the basis for their skits and musical numbers. The use of fresh news for cabaret numbers is more a German than an American pastime although, in recent years, Mort Sahl and Lenny Bruce used the daily papers as the basis for many of their nightclub routines. In the United States, genial works like *Pins and Needles* and *The Cradle Will Rock*, which had an amateur air in their origin and production, combined a general vitality with an episodic character with no large and dominant focus. Their bite was, if not quite toothless, rarely more than nippy.

Social comment in the United States during the Depression emerged in the form of ingratiating musical evenings, only mildly spiced, rather than as more seriously disturbing operatic attempts, like those of Bertolt Brecht in Germany. Works like Elmer Rice's *Street Scene* or Maxwell Anderson's *Winterset* or Lillian Hellman's *The Little Foxes*, all of which would seem to lend themselves originally to operatic treatment and indeed did so at later times, were conceived of first in the black-and-white form of straight drama. Although there were more than enough bitter and angry things to be said in the formal American dramatic theatre, somehow musical drama, even under the benevolent auspices of the Federal Theatre, which did sponsor some angry texts, did not address itself to the same sort of subject. The implicit intention of the musical theatre of the twenties, to provide pretty spectacle, exotic settings, catchy melody, a general sumptuousness, all of these seemed to keep guiding the musical drama even in the thirties. (Nor has the musical spectacle of the twenties been displaced in the American scene: it survives in full vigor in New York's Radio City Music Hall and in Las Vegas, in such productions as those of the Lido and the Folies Bergère companies. The audiences have simply changed, from the urban to the provincial; the Music Hall's patrons are overwhelmingly out-of-town visitors and/or local provincials.)

Nevertheless, the peculiarly political intention, the "liberal" impulse, implicit in political satire (can there ever be a "conservative" political satire?), determined the direction and the character that important American musical drama was to take in the next several decades, in subject matter, in technique, and even in stagecraft.

The musical innovativeness of works like *Pins and Needles* and *The Cradle Will Rock* and the WPA Theatre's *The Hot Mikado*, a jazz rendition by a Negro troupe of the original Gilbert and Sullivan work, suggested some of the devices that musical comedy might exploit in its escape from the pseudo-operatic music and dance of Sigmund Romberg. A new audience, in short, had clearly been developed to respond to the several delights of an integrated text, songs, music, and dance offered by a work like *Oklahoma!*

Now *Oklahoma!* for all of its originality and freshness, was insured against failure, at least, by its incorporating qualities of the semioperatic Romberg variety as well as those of the new musical theatre. It was set in a moderately exotic territory, remote in place and time, Oklahoma at the beginning of the century; its people were colorful peasants, dressed in the native costume of the area, a kind of joke since the cowboy outfit was not unfamiliar to American audiences brought up to worship Tom Mix, Hoot Gibson, Ken Maynard, Buck Jones, and other such heroes; the plot was simple, engaging, with only the barest hint of the serious or dark, the presence of the sinister Jud, enough to suggest an area of reality but not enough to explore it. Most significantly, perhaps, positively to insure success, was the revolutionary quality of the dance numbers as well as the folklike character of the principals and their affairs. Those perceptive critics who derided the fake folk art of *Oklahoma!* caught the artificiality; the point, of course, was that this very artificiality was there to appeal to the Popular Front expectations of the new audience, an audience attuned to the beginnings of the contemporary revival of folk music in the performances of Burl Ives, Pete Seeger, John Jacob Niles, Richard Dyer-Bennett, and Josh White. There was even in the body of the work a specific leftist slogan, in the song declaring that the farmer and the cowhand shall be friends.

The works following *Oklahoma!* by Rodgers and Hammerstein were not so innovative technically, but they continued to use materials calculated to appeal to the liberal ear, mind, and general taste. *South Pacific* incorporates as part of its plotting the reconciliation of different cultures, positions, and points of view, in its delicate handling of miscegenation and the issue of marriage between youthful and older persons, and in its suggestion that the American occupation of the Pacific islands was in itself an enlightening enterprise, both for the Americans and for the natives. *The King and I* is, among other things, an account of several conflicts: between cultures, an enlightened Western one and a primitive Eastern one; between classes; and between sexes. The thrust is to suggest the final, Messianic mingling of one world, one culture, in which we all give ourselves over to the pleasures of getting to know one another.

The liberal expectation of musical drama was that innovation in technique was to be welcomed, almost in and of itself: immediately attractive novelty of form, whether deceptive or genuine in its effort at originality, proved the breaking away from the conservative and established. But no choreographic, musical, or textual innovation should put a burden of understanding or appreciation on the theatregoer: nothing should be so radical as to puzzle or confuse. Certain expectations still had to be met. *On the Town*, then, was very tentative in its blending of basic jazz and easier musical idioms, both classical and popular (without ever descending obviously to the *kitsch* of the semiclassical). The dance numbers, by Jerome Robbins, continued the Agnes De Mille manner of turning into classical ballet forms the gestures and movements common to such familiar proletariat cultural groups as cowboys and sailors. In *Damn Yankees*, the ballet sequences are based on the movements of baseball players; in *How to Succeed in Business without Really Trying*, they are based on those of office typists and clerks; in *Company*, on simple domestic movements.

But technical experimenting and breakthrough soon reached a point of diminishing returns. There was only so much that might be done with music or with dance or with setting without breaking into truly strange territory. More and more, musicals derived from earlier successes; the writers and composers plagiarized themselves. The De Mille and the Robbins choreographic signatures became as familiar and readily identifiable as the lyrics of Cole Porter, Irving Berlin, or Frank Loesser. The newer dance movements introduced from England in the sixties on such television programs as "Hullabaloo!" were too daring, too bizarre, to be early incorporated into the commercial theatre, dependent, like all American business, on mass production and mass consumption.

As American musical comedy looked inside the darker depths of American society for its subject matter, instead of to Graustark and to other nonexistent and bright faraway places, it did so not with the object of using music to intensify a searching self-examination, but to make pretty, to sugarcoat, to make palatable what might otherwise be essentially distasteful and, even, uncomfortable. Consequently no subject, properly dressed up, was inappropriate for musical comedy. *Pal Joey* is an account of an affair between a pimp and gigolo, and a call girl. *Guys and Dolls* is a happy musical comedy principally about Broadway drifters, pool hall sharks, gamblers, gangsters, whores, and a stray Salvation Army lass, presumably to provide a point of reference by extreme contrast: actually, she only proves that "good hearts" are universal (Salvation Army ladies have become almost figures of myth, in *Major Barbara, Saint Joan of the Stockyards,* and *The Connection*). *Fiorello!,* based on the career of one of the truly heroic municipal politicians in the United States, happily incorporates a subplot about the New York City Hall scandals involving the private tin boxes in which various politicians deposited their graft receipts. Any intentional sardonic quality comes only from the acting and directing. *Li'l Abner* is another light and ebullient musical, about, of all things, illiterate hillbillies, presumably from Appalachia.

Perhaps the most spectacular feat of making an unpleasant past both pretty and even instructive occurs in the context of *The King and I,* where Harriet Beecher Stowe's antislavery novel, *Uncle Tom's Cabin,* is rendered into an engaging children's ballet, called "The Small House of Uncle Thomas," in which the narrative and the dance numbers have become stylized by way of Siamese gestures and speech patterns. The hunting of Eliza across the ice floes by the bloodhounds is used as the occasion for some charming dance steps and ingenious stage effects. American slavery with its accompanying brutality and disregard for human values thus becomes sweet. The point of the ballet in context, of course, is to persuade the Siamese king against separating two young lovers, one of whom is scheduled to be sent into slavery. But the king is unmoved. Indeed, he is angered at the suggestion that this pretty fantasy should control him and his immediately real world. Anna's hope here, to change an ugly situation through the insidious power of art, is noble, certainly, but quixotic, perhaps even analogous to the intentions of some musical comedy producers themselves.

It is remarkable that with all of the Negro talent for

so long available to the Broadway theatre, both of singers and dancers, so little use has been made of material involving miscegenation, so long a national obsession. The musical version of Clifford Odets's *Golden Boy* with Sammy Davis is perhaps the most striking fulfillment, at least in bare intention, of the latent possibility in this still uncomfortable subject, but *No Strings*, the Richard Rodgers musical, is a more typical, stylized, and prettified evasion: the black and white lovers do not marry.

In effect, then, musical comedy was returning, very nearly full circle, to the Graustarkian flights of the twenties. Witness *Promenade*, with its ironic, nostalgic use of that time. A familiar enough ugly neighborhood was blurred over with attractive, insulating sounds and colors. As in so much liberalistic art, we could satisfy our social sense that we were doing the right thing in simply stating the objectionable, without at the same time developing the need to be stirred to any other response, like trying to change anything, or even to recognize anything in its plain ugliness. The problem of ethnic hostility, at the heart of *West Side Story*, could be transmuted into the simple longing inherent in a song like "Maria," a longing perhaps not very different from that embodied in a Nelson Eddy–Jeanette MacDonald duet. The very real social distress that gave the work its initial cogency thus becomes subdued, diverted, in the interest of entertainment, in our eternal if worn concern with young lovers. The conflict between the young men and the police turns *merely* into a comic song. The operative dynamic is that it is better to have a problem stated even in a highly distorted but attractive way than not to have it stated at all. One can deceive himself for the moment into believing that he has actually considered the problem of the Puerto Rican minority in New York City, in *West Side Story*, by attending to the bittersweet Romeo-and-Juliet affair of the lovers, or to the street-gang rivalries, without ever actually confronting any more than this. *No Strings* provides the satisfaction of thinking that we have actually had examined for us the problem of racial intermarriage.

Nevertheless, the trend to adapting socially disturbing subjects for musical drama did provide a new body of substantive material with which to nourish new growths and lay out new directions in musical comedy. *The Threepenny Opera*, for example, introduced the Brechtian possibility. The American version of the original *Die Dreigroschenoper* was a highly sanitary, cleansed, decorated rendition of unpleasant characters, setting, and activities. Where, for example, the original German cast sang the very catchy material in coarse, cacophonous tones, the American singers were smooth and pleasing. The paradox had its own curious validity: there is something especially chilling in hearing Mack the Knife's songs rendered in a mellifluous, attractive voice; the original German does not provide this tension between the content and the style. But it is finally too easily possible, for someone unwary, to miss the undertone of horror which characterizes the German original.

After World War II, the various theatres of the absurd, of anger, of the nonheroic developed and blended in various forms. While we continued to have our share of musical comedies in which the central figure was in some measure an object of envy and emulation, as in *Mame* or in *Hello, Dolly!*, equally popular works were those about antiheroes, like *Man of La Mancha*, Don Quixote emerging as a curiously modern man, and works in which there is not so much a single hero as a "heroic" situation which verges on the edge of tragedy: *Fiddler on the Roof* and *Cabaret*. Black humor was to be found not only in the nightclub routines of Lenny Bruce and

Jonathan Winters but in works like *Auntie Mame,* both the original and the musical version, *Mame,* about a bohemian eccentric in the twenties and thirties, whose activities had a rather somber undertone of self-indulgent kookiness. It is difficult to take *Mame* too seriously, simply because the brush strokes of wackiness are too broad, too little shaded to suggest the sadness under the zaniness. Auntie Mame is no Groucho Marx, who is, after all, a detached comic commentator; neither is she a *Man of La Mancha,* however self-deceivingly involved. She takes her idiosyncrasies at the same time too seriously and too lightly. Mary McCarthy's effort to record the intensity of emotional commitment in the same world, in *The Group,* indicates the larger dimension of frustration in which *Mame* might have been depicted. *Mame* and *Hello, Dolly!,* polished studies in evasion, nevertheless hint at bleak possibilities.

It is in the tragic Jewish backgrounds of *Fiddler on the Roof* and of *Cabaret,* however, where we may find the newest modes, in the gingerly mixing of the sad and joyous, allowing us to escape yet not escape, to enjoy and to suffer. The gallows humor of Sholom Aleichem has been turned into dark unsweetened chocolate bonbons for Hadassah–Helen Hokinson ladies: after all, too much sugar isn't good for the figure. Here, as in earlier musical comedies about essentially uncomfortable subjects, the quite dismal past of the East European Jews has been blurred by a sentimentalizing nostalgia turned into a Marc Chagall collage of dreamlike images, isolated, floating, rendered attractive by memory since, clearly, we have not only survived but have triumphed to the extent of being able to review this dismal past in the comfort of this very Broadway theatre. But the memories of the poverty and of the pogroms persist, underneath all that pretty fiddling, singing, and dancing.

Cabaret is even more ambivalent and, perhaps as a

result, more successful as an instance of the new American musical comedy. It does not try to make other than awful the details of pre-Nazi nightclub life. The painted androgyne, the satanic or at least Mephistophelian master of ceremonies, immediately establishes the gruesome character of the events. The hefty chorus line which hides in its midst a male and makes its exit goose-stepping produces a gasp simultaneously with a laugh. The American heroine scarcely summons any genuine sympathy since her shallowness is so totally congenital: there is no fall in her progress. Her two-dimensionality is inviolate. Nor do the other characters, some of whom are indeed ingratiating but also very familiar, summon much sympathy.

What is memorably perverse, finally, about *Cabaret* is that two of the catchiest numbers, the two that perhaps most concisely embody the theme of the activities, the ones most properly belonging to the repertory of popular music, are exactly those that are most disturbingly unsubtle. The title song simply invites you to come to the cabaret, the club in microcosm of all of the vulgarity, shallow, self-stimulated passion, brutality masquerading as feeling, which characterized pre-Hitler Berlin. The other, a delicate fuguelike melody, sung by a chorus of waiters, is a celebration of Nazism. Perhaps the only hint of the ambiguity of this song is that the solo part is sung by what sounds like a castrato.

The appeal of a work like *Cabaret* is ambivalent: it entertains the audience with exactly the kind of material, in dance number and in text, that should offend it. It is thus a very oblique insult when it works. When it does not work, that is, when one catches the documentary ugliness of what is going on, when one responds to the activity and to the atmosphere as though one were actually sitting in a Berlin nightclub of the late twenties, or in the stadium at Nuremberg during one of Hitler's speeches, repelled and paralyzed, it does not work so well since it is not at all clear that there is the necessary satiric control. It is document, not caricature. That is, quite simply, this work could be produced in a sympathetic Nazi atmosphere today without disturbing any members of that audience. For us, the joke resides in the fact that the producers and other persons associated with the shaping of the show happen to be Jewish, and it is being observed safely in a more or less safe America. A comparable "joke" might be contrived by having a road company production of *Fiddler on the Roof* done, say, by Arabs in an Arab country, or by Nazi sympathizers in Lower Bavaria. In short, the ambivalent thrust of the text depends too much on a performance. For all one might make out from the bare libretto and words, this could be a nostalgic German musical comedy—to the extent that civilized Germans would allow themselves such a pleasantry today.

Cabaret does have the quality of an assault, on an American or English audience at least, and this quality is certainly related to such pioneering musical attempts as *Your Own Thing*, *Hair*, and *Viet Rock*. These more clearly pierce through our defensive expectations to be delighted by musical comedy. *Hair* especially derives from Olsen and Johnson, who, in their revues, literally afflicted the audience in various harmless physical ways, or from the work of nightclub and burlesque-house comedians who pick on members of the audience to stir up and insult. *Hair* and *Oh! Calcutta!*, with their nudity and explicit sexual activity, are indeed closely related to the exhibitions of nakedness in burlesque grind houses or at illicit stag shows: what other form of theatre has such a calculatedly practical end as the sexual excitation of the audience (whether the end is fully achieved or not)? This is a form of the ultimately liberal. *Promises, Promises*, superficially resembling conventional Broadway musical comedy, is "liberal" at least in its black humor, deriving ultimately from the sardonic, Brechtian view of its film original, *The Apartment. Company* ironically celebrates prolonged bachelorhood simultaneously with the pretences of contemporary proper domesticity.

Musical comedy, renewing its vitality off-Broadway, is becoming another form in the new American drama involving the audience more totally in the theatrical experience. Even this has something of community sings about it, mixing union hall, political rally, and church affair. But the power of music to charm can also move and shock, and the theatre of involvement will more and more be incorporating the current musical idioms in its total arsenal.

6

Will Success Spoil the American Dramatist?

The dramatist has always clearly had a problem different from that of the poet or of the writer of fiction. Poets and novelists may survive for long periods on succès d'estime only, meaningful critical or editorial response that encourages continued work. Playwrights must have popular success as well; they obviously must work in a large social situation, with actors, directors, critics, and audiences. What this has come to mean is that few serious American writers who have cared to succeed in the theatre have felt that they could afford the "luxury" more common to the poet or novelist, that of ultimately pleasing themselves. (Not that pleasing oneself always leads to worthy results: one may have low ambitions; but deliberately not doing so can rarely lead to anything worth very much.)

The piquant account is relevant here of Saul Bellow's failure with his first play, *The Last Analysis*, in 1964, at the same time that his novel, *Herzog*, was achieving great critical and popular success. Bellow reported that he allowed director, producer, and actors to keep changing the text of the play since he wanted to make a killing and was ready to heed any advice of experienced persons that might conceivably help. On the other hand, he felt certain that his novel would not satisfy a large audience and so he strictly resisted editorial changes: if few were going to read his novel anyway, at least it would remain exactly as he wrote it.

Obviously accommodation to professional demands need not be fatal to Broadway success: William Gibson recorded at length how his play *Two for the Seesaw* was tailored to satisfy production specialists of various sorts; it was a satisfactory commercial success. Gibson wrote about his experience: "Fifteen years earlier, when my work consisted of unpublished poems and a magazine asked me to change a word in one, I would not change the word; the poem went unpublished; it was a far cry to the present spate of rewriting to please." Such shaping has become one of the background specialties in the American theatre; witness the profession of "play doctoring," especially for musical comedies, the technique of bringing in some expert, in dialogue or in building a situation, to resuscitate an ailing work on out-of-town tryouts.

For many American writers the theatre has come to be the main arena to achieve the fullest measure of literary success, perhaps precisely because of its more social character. But the theatre, while it has attracted writers who were first novelists, seems at the same time to have inhibited and intimidated them, very possibly because of the expectations the theatre establishes. Henry James's efforts to write a successful play were as strenuous as they were futile; Hemingway, a master of dialogue, brought off the remarkable feat of embodying probably his worst writing in a play, *The Fifth Column*; William Faulkner buried a closet drama in a novel, *Requiem for a Nun*, later to be made into a successful work for the French theatre by Albert Camus.

John O'Hara wrote ingenuously about his own wish to write plays. He became famous and wealthy through his novels, short stories, and film scripts; he had been taken seriously enough, in academic and in respectable literary circles, particularly for his short fiction, to have evoked scholarly and critical study and to have received esteemed literary acclaim. In the introduction to his collection of *Five Plays*, none of them ever commercially produced with financial success, he spoke here and there of the profit motive in writing, and what is most revealing about his comments is the intimation that a director's help *would* have been welcome if it somehow "guaranteed" a hit. It's the hit that matters; and, indeed, in *The Champagne Pool*, one of the five plays in the volume, a successful playwright does indicate gratitude to a knowing director. O'Hara made evident, however indirectly, that "success," a hit, cancelled out any ugliness of compromise.

American drama has for so long been Broadway drama, that is, financially successful drama, that no writer can think of a "hit," with all it implies of the importance of drama critics' reviews, long runs, large audiences, theatre parties, Hollywood bids for the movie rights, without having in mind those financial aspects of success that sometimes blur or obliterate the other aspects of achievement. From the Provincetown Playhouse of around 1920 to the San Francisco Actors Workshop of the 1960s, artistically ambitious and successful American drama has led directly to Broadway. Provincetown "fulfilled its promise" and its efforts with the Theatre Guild and Eugene O'Neill; the directors of the serious, energetic, ambitious San Francisco group, Herbert Blau and Jules Irving, went to the Lincoln Repertory Theatre in New York, only a step or two from Broadway (where, unhappily, they did not sustain or fulfill the promise of the Workshop). The costs of putting on a Broadway play have increased so fantastically since the end of World War II that only a Croesus could afford to ignore financial considerations. Two contrasts, cited by Eric Bentley: *Life with Father* (1939) cost $23,000 to produce;

Life with Mother (1948), $85,000. A prewar Saroyan play cost $5,000; a postwar Williams play, $115,000.

During the great economic depression of the thirties, "success" as measured simply by money became somewhat meaningless. Serious drama and serious workers in the theatre would have suffered virtual extinction of their careers but for the formation of government-sponsored groups like the Federal Theatre, especially the Mercury players under Orson Welles, and of private ones, like the Group Theatre. Released from the pressures to be conventionally "successful," these groups were free to work with repertory or with experiments (a jazz version of *Macbeth*; a Fascist-uniformed *Julius Caesar*; the "living newspaper" documentaries, like *One Third of a Nation*; the social realism of Odets). A small number of individual playwrights with organized leftist support could find backing for plays on something like the plight of the Scottsboro boys, the young southern Negroes who would have been judicially lynched but for the intervention of northern lawyers supported by the Party. In short, in the thirties an American drama seemed to be developing that was not governed mainly by "success."

But the subsequent careers of the various personages connected with these ventures emphasizes the determining force of "success." As the United States climbed out of the Depression, almost without exception everyone—from Odets, the writer, through Franchot Tone and John Garfield, the actors, to the directors and producers of the Federal Theatre, the Group Theatre, and the privately sponsored productions —moved on, more or less permanently, to Hollywood and the massive salaries of the films. Perhaps Harold Clurman alone was the most significant figure who remained working principally in the theatre, as director and critic.

This pragmatic measure for the American dramatist has had various results over the years. It has meant, for one thing, that, with the glaring exception of O'Neill, we have had no writer who has continued to produce for the stage a body of work that approaches in substance and variety the work of contemporaries in Europe— Brecht, Pirandello, Lorca, Anouilh. The successful American playwright is honored by being given every chance not to write plays again, much as in the academic world the "successful" professor is taken out of the classroom altogether. Clifford Odets is our most famous instance of the dramatist diverted from the theatre by Hollywood and television contracts (where he turned out workmanlike but not memorable scripts); more recently, Paddy Chayefsky, whose Broadway plays had not even had a chance yet to add up to the promise, let alone the fulfillment of Odets, has left the theatre; and others. Perhaps there is a sense of "reward" here for work well done on Broadway by the offer of the passport to Hollywood, the chance to retire to Stratford to live like a gentleman with a veritable coat of arms. Frederick Loewe, the composer of the music for *My Fair Lady*, *Camelot*, and some lesser known but equally estimable works before these, announced from his yacht in the Mediterranean more than once, as if to reassure himself, that he would never write a note again since he was now wealthy enough never to have to do so. After success, what?

But it is likely that writing for the theatre has always been determined by matters of market, of competition (rivalries between theatrical groups, for example, in Elizabethan and Restoration England), of pressures of various sorts, even aesthetic ones, to pick up the idiom of the new fiction, say, or of films, or of television. In the United States, the pressure of "success" has dominated over other pressures, even to the shaping of the text, to the determining (sometimes unconsciously) of subject matter.

Edward Albee's main talent, for instance, probably

still lies, as does Ionesco's, and perhaps Pinter's, in short, tight, one-act plays. But Broadway has never been hospitable to the one-acter. After his success off-Broadway with *The American Dream*, *The Zoo Story*, *The Sandbox*, *The Death of Bessie Smith*, all tightly vignetted one-act plays, Albee moved on to Broadway with his sprawling, enormous work, *Who's Afraid of Virginia Woolf?* It has been hugely successful in the usual American terms: much money, several road companies, film rights, fame, the accompanying revival of interest in his earlier short plays. The point is that, whether or not we think *Virginia Woolf* a good play, I doubt that we would have had it at all but for its length, a prerequisite for Broadway investment and production.

From the twenties, when the theatre in America first began to have a stature comparable to that of the theatre in Europe, the theme of success has permeated the subject matter of our most important playwrights. Themselves so rigorously controlled by success, they often seemed obsessed by the power, both creative and destructive, of success in the larger American landscape. George Kelly's *The Show-Off* is about a common American type, the grown man who always boasts of imaginary achievements beyond his capacity or his understanding. His *Craig's Wife* is about a woman whose notion of marriage—indeed, of life—is to present the façade of perfection and to maintain it, to offer to the neighbors, her audience, a fixed landscape of success, in her sterile marriage, in the frozen finality of her household interior.

In the thirties, successful serious drama was politically oriented, specifically leftist. But, even when success was realistically a most distant chimera, a play like *Awake and Sing* recorded as the major ambition of the characters their longing for the middle-class images of success: a decent income with the perquisites that flow from it (marriage, a home)—almost simply that and little more. The title would seem to call for more than a mere ascension from poverty and defeat, arise and sing, a reaching for some private, ecstatic, human fulfillment, but the text modestly limits itself to "success" alone. Good enough, certainly, as a start for singing, but it is the end, the climax. In Arthur Miller's *Death of a Salesman*, all that Willy Loman wants is the middle-class apotheosis of success: a mortgage paid off, a car clear of debt, a properly working modern refrigerator, an occasional mistress, sons "well-liked" if uneducated and aimless. Willy Loman is Babbitt, twenty years later.

The plays of Tennessee Williams are dominated by an atmosphere of un-success and anti-success, which may be part of their total perverseness, a denial of the main American impulses of ambition and fulfillment. Tom Wingfield in *The Glass Menagerie* and his sister and mother are impotent in making their way in the larger world, from which they escape to their several private refuges. His mother dreams of her youthful successes as a southern belle, distant conquests that live ideally in the memory only, with no blemishes of reality or of fact. Stanley Kowalski in *A Streetcar Named Desire* scorns the substance and the surface of clean, properly spoken, middle-class American success, scorns the pride that comes with family lineage. Himself proud only of his greasy, dirty proletarian work and appearance and speech, his whole bearing a defiance of the usual accouterments of success, he systematically sets out to destroy the barely flickering spark of family pride, perhaps the only success she has ever known, which sustains Blanche Dubois, his sister-in-law. Williams's later works frequently include as critical incidents the physical decay or a physical assault and consequent maiming, directly or indirectly sexual, of successful, even heroic figures.

Our serious playwrights, while they remain in the theatre, sooner or later get down to the matter of success in something of its ambiguities and perplexities. Odets in *Paradise Lost*, one of his later plays, relates success to bankruptcy, death, disease. The hero, sums up Malcolm Goldstein, "has lost the paradise of the middle class, but has found a better life among the homeless proletariat." Odets, ironically, anticipated Williams in finding "success" through rejecting middle-class ways and values.

Miller in *After the Fall* provides an uncomfortably clinical dissection of several aspects of American success, which we know, as we come to the play, he has achieved himself in plenitude: that fame that allows the "successful" intellectual, the archetypal hero of the intelligentsia for the fashionable moment, to carry off into marriage the archetypal American beauty queen; the fame that provides, through money and self-confidence, ready escape by divorce from early and unglamorous marriage; that enables one, through the excuse of the demands of worldly importance, to neglect the ordinary fidelities asserted by family; to neglect, as convenient, one's other identities, the force of friendships, or of being Jewish: success raises one to a level of social functioning where the routine mortal amenities are beside or below the point. *After the Fall* is "clinical" because, in spite of its patent wish to find absolution, it is relentless in its exposure.

Guilt accompanies success in America; some of our best writers are driven to excesses of apologia, destructive self-examinations under the pressures of success, denying it, explaining it away, even mutilating it. Ambition and the fulfillment of ambition are still to be apologized for; a satisfactory climax after energy expended, still to be denied or explained away; no time to relax with the pleasure of work or play well done, our vestigial Puritanism asserting its dominance. Arnold Weinstein in *The Red Eye of Love* (1962) burlesques the American lust for success (the main character is an indefatigable inventor, neglecting wife and child, developing a doll that will get sick, run a temperature, and eventually die so that he can then market a flood of medical and funeral toys to sell with the doll) at the same time that he offers in his dramaturgy an anthology of successful vaudeville, burlesque-house, and movie techniques: slapstick routines, quick shifts of scene, silly wordplay, top-banana and straight-man skits.

O'Neill's power derived in good measure from his capacity to go his own way, which was to try one way after another. He remained a dramatist, not simply because he could afford to, but because he had to: it is ludicrous to imagine an O'Neill in Hollywood or working for television. (Faulkner, of course, did go to Hollywood, but he never accommodated comfortably. He became a Hollywood legend rather than a film writer; he had no significant screen credits to himself.) Although O'Neill in his adult work was perhaps less conditioned than other writers of his generation by the usual pressures of American success, the initial conditioning had already worked its effects. O'Neill's career of working with various forms and themes culminated in the mighty *Long Day's Journey into Night*, published and produced posthumously, which is the lucid and bitter record of how O'Neill's actor-father sowed the seeds of Gene's physical and perhaps psychological ill-health and general wretchedness in a life-long compulsive drive to amass and keep a fortune. O'Neill, at least in his earlier years, kept providing American audiences what they seemed to want at one time or another.

The very fact that American drama has had to satisfy particular large audiences at particular times has meant that in some way successful plays have articulated, however obliquely, social needs or responses of various depths. A long-running play like *Abie's Irish Rose*, which

began its career in the twenties, like the dialect vaudeville comedians of the time, with their Yiddish, German,
Irish, and Italian accents, surely had something to do
with the coming to maturity of the children of immigrants of various backgrounds. Indeed, the play recorded a particularly dreadful union in reality, an
Orthodox Jewish and an Irish Catholic pairing: the
memories of pogroms were still vivid among Jewish
immigrants from East Europe; the Christian peasant's
superstitious dread of secret Jewish blood rituals was
equally vivid. Yet the text was trivial, sentimental,
straining after comic effect, mixing accents, making the
most out of the obvious incongruities and ironies. Black-
face minstrel shows, seemingly innocent and vastly
popular American entertainment throughout the un-
tutored areas of the country that Mencken once described as a cultural Sahara, had their roots in slavery;
they lurk behind the sinister surface of T. S. Eliot's
Sweeney Agonistes. American drama brings up from the
depths hidden, repressed, suppressed preoccupations and
terrors, but then renders them innocuous in the interest
of "success."

Two of the most successful plays of the twenties,
Maxwell Anderson and Laurence Stallings's *What Price
Glory?* and Ben Hecht and Charles MacArthur's *The
Front Page*, recorded the adolescent camaraderie of
masculine milieus, the war front, a newspaper office,
where women were demeaned or excluded. They are
innocent enough records of that unconscious homo-
sexuality in American life that Norman Mailer makes
such a fuss about "exposing." And Mrs. Craig systematically tried to impose her vengeful sterility on her
male-dominated world. We can too easily oversimplify
the complexities of the context in which these plays
appeared, but, without saying more, it may be enough
for the moment to note that in the twenties women

were beginning to enter and make their way in the full American scene.

Odets recorded the bitterness of resignation during the thirties of a straining middle class to achieve some significant measure of American "success." That the families he depicted were primarily Jewish and matriarchal reflected a larger American preoccupation, hinted at in the matriarchal family of John Steinbeck's *The Grapes of Wrath*, more clearly enunciated in the wide popularity of Jewish themes in the fifties and sixties. Jewish ambitions and situations (in Odets, Miller, Kopit, and Albee), so deeply puritanical and family oriented, were crystallized distillates of larger American sensitivities. The overprotective, emasculating Jewish mother (Bessie Berger in *Awake and Sing*) found her counterpart in the greater American mother (Mom of *The American Dream*). Jewish "momism" anticipated the larger national Momism uncovered by such different observers as Philip Wylie and Geoffrey Gorer. (Gorer went so far as to relate the American fascination with bare bosoms in advertisements, the movies, musical comedies, burlesque houses, and magazines to a continual need throughout adulthood for maternal breast feeding.)

Arthur Miller's largest success has resided possibly in his uncanny talent to keep attuned simultaneously to both the loud and the subdued melodies of American life. *All My Sons*, a play about a businessman's greed during World War II, was written, as Miller tells us in the introduction to his collected plays, to examine the area of widespread moral ambivalence towards the sacrifices everyone was supposed to be making; trivial and large cheating was commonplace. The suggestion was that business success during war could somehow only have been immoral and criminal; the suggestion received a wide welcome. *The Crucible* caught the country's sense of bewilderment and fright during the McCarthy era.

Death of a Salesman, still probably Miller's best play, is built around more subtle, more amorphous themes, and consequently more significant ones: the surviving sense of insecurity even after the New Deal among the middle classes whose fathers still had to sell themselves. Willy Loman, desperately wanting an "American" identity (to be well-liked, to have a football hero for a son), cannot accept himself (apparently Jewish, he never alludes to the substantive implications of this fact), cannot see that veneer alone wears down and vanishes (he does nothing to give his sons those roots in education, for example, which, the play makes clear through the career of Bernard, their cousin, are necessary to a real American success). Willy never blames himself for anything: destruction comes from out there and is always unjust.

For many in the audiences of the late forties and early fifties, the period of greatest success of the play, Willy Loman's groping for stability and status mirrored their own attempts to establish a rooted identity in the uncertain post-Depression and postwar landscape.

Miller was early obsessed by the role "success" plays in molding destiny in America. In the introduction to his collected plays, he writes about a "desk-drawer" play, later to be produced for four nights, *The Man Who Had All the Luck,* which he describes as a failure:

This play was an investigation to discover what exact part a man played in his own fate. It deals with a young man in a small town who, by the time he is in his mid-twenties owns several growing businesses, has married the girl he loves, is the father of a child he has always wanted, and is daily becoming convinced that as his desires are gratified he is causing to accumulate around his own head an invisible but nearly palpable fund, so to speak, of retribution. The law of life, as he observes life around him, is that people are always frustrated in some important regard; and he conceives that he must be too, and the play is built around his conviction of impending disaster. The disaster never comes, even when, in effect, he tries to bring it on in order to survive it and find peace. Instead, he comes to believe in his remarkable ability to succeed.

Miller concludes his résumé of *The Man Who Had All the Luck* by remarking that it is now possible for him "to see that far from being a waste and a failure this play was a preparation, and possibly a necessary one, for those that followed, especially *All My Sons* and *Death of a Salesman*." The first records the destruction that comes to the successful man in America, for success came to him only through criminality; the second records the destruction that comes to the unsuccessful man who has dedicated himself to pursuing only the appearances of American success.

Early in the century William Dean Howells, the American novelist, critic, and editor, suggested that British drama of the time differed from American in being concerned with larger, social contexts rather than with smaller, domestic ones. Surely this is an oversimplification, and one that has gone through many modulations over the decades, but it may still be somewhere near the heart of the mystery accounting for the importance of success in the American theatre. Theatre-going in America has always been a somewhat different sociological phenomenon from that in other countries. The earnings of our jolly musicals alone would demonstrate that American theatre is before anything else a form of entertainment, in the company, say, of the circus, state fairs, and athletic contests. Critics have argued that American drama cannot be "literature" because it has, first, to be "likable," to "please," and pleasure is here served best by sentimental evasions, the appearances of boldness and independence, opportunities for the audience to identify itself with characters and causes but in no disturbing sense.

Thus, it is easier for American audiences in the sixties to confront the Negro question, North or South, through the familial pleasantness of Lorraine Hansberry's *A Raisin in the Sun*, rather than through the socially sweeping and brutal James Baldwin's *Blues for Mr. Charlie* or the sustained insult of LeRoi Jones's *Dutchman* (in which a white girl, after flirting with a Negro young man on the New York subway, stabs him to death when he asserts his "independence" to be whatever he wants to be, including an imitation of a white contemporary). According to this view, the fact that *A Raisin in the Sun* is a cleaner and more coherent piece of craftsmanship than the other two works (all by Negro writers) has less to do with its success than its attractive surface. William Saroyan's *The Time of Your Life* gets through to us better than Eugene O'Neill's *The Iceman Cometh*, with which it has thematic and dramaturgic relations, because of its greater sentimentality and warmth. It is certainly true that O'Neill's work strives for a larger, symbolic mysteriousness than the momentary, boozy divertissements of a saloon hospitable to assorted odd characters. Elmer Rice's domestic epic, *Street Scene*, is more memorable than his *Adding Machine*, a comment on the mechanization of modern man. William Inge's husbands, wives, and children are far less abrasive than Edward Albee's or Tennessee Williams's families; Inge has "delighted" more audiences than Albee and Williams.

There is a continuum in American "dramatic" entertaining from the most popular forms (vaudeville and burlesque dialogues, radio and television's thin melodramas, Hollywood slapstick or domestic comedies and westerns, staged bad-guy-versus-good-guy wrestling matches, rock-'n'-roll singing, even circuses and cowboy rodeos) to the more cultivated, less popular ones (opera and theatre). There have been many attempts, indeed, to link the two extremes; as has been remarked, the choreography of a number of semioperatic musicals has been based on the movements of cowboys, baseball players, or of Mack Sennett's Keystone Cops. It seems to me unresponsive to actuality to insist that popular forms have only blunted the effectiveness of our more serious forms. Indeed, it may be that we can sometimes examine the point and character of success in our serious drama by considering appropriately our frivolous entertainment.

O'Neill, as we have seen, has long posed a problem to serious American critics. O'Neill is certainly anything but ingratiating. He requires effort. Why? I suggest that it is precisely because of his intensity of concentration on an issue, on a form, on a text—almost without regard to the relation of the work to an audience, to its performance as a *theatrical* experience. It may well be that his great, fumbling inarticulateness, or, at best, fuzzy articulateness, has something to do with a greater American inchoateness, a greater American incapacity to come down in some traditional manner to tight and sharp fundamentals, a groping for self-justifying transcendental formulations; but I think it is his conscious, willed, controlled unawareness of, indifference to, audiences that accounts for the extravagance of his effects, both the successes and the failures.

In actuality, America is a collection of audiences, ranging enormously in its preparation for certain entertainments (New York dudes are as baffled by rodeos as cowboy primitives might be by opera), but in essence more linked than any two excessively divergent groups are likely to concede. Consider a rodeo audience somewhere out West as opposed to a small group in Greenwich Village viewing Jack Gelber's avant-garde *The Connection*, a play showing a group of addicts, including a jazz combo, waiting to make connection with their supplier of heroin. Both are involved, as Lionel Abel put it in his essay on the play in *Metatheatre* (1963), in making a "connection," in becoming involved in the activities going on, in finding a moment of special meaning to themselves. Americans "participate" with remarkable suspension of disbelief; they identify with and, not infrequently, themselves join the action. It was during a New York performance of Osborne's *Look Back in Anger* that a lady in the audience is said to have rushed onstage to belabor Jimmy Porter with an umbrella for his ugly treatment of his wife.

American drama may be especially difficult, for native or foreign critics, to grasp in anything like its entirety because the tendency is to neglect or ignore or disdain certain obscure areas. Eric Bentley has commented about American critics that though "they know something of literature . . . they are anti-literary; they are pro-theatrical but know little of acting." Not only do American students of the drama frequently fail to connect the theatrical with the literary, but in emphasizing the literary so exclusively, they frequently fail to see the drama in its larger social context. One example of neglect is the career of Gertrude Berg, who in the twenties was the leading actress and, from time to time, one of the writers of the radio and television serial, "The Rise of the Goldbergs," that went on almost as long as "Amos 'n' Andy," another "ethnic" entertainment, about Negroes. Before her death, Mrs. Berg went through one popular matinee drama after another on

Broadway, one of them with Sir Cedric Hardwicke, in which he played a Japanese gentleman and she an Orthodox Jewish widow from the Bronx who married him. Her continued popularity, especially with the Jewish middle-class matrons of New York and the surrounding areas, who largely make up the matinee audiences of Broadway, suggested that there was a significant element of identification of audiences with her, and with the characters she portrayed, involved in her success. It may also tell us something about the folksiness requisite to a larger theatrical success in this country, the meeting of expectations that may be simple and conscious (to hear a funny story, to see a pleasing turn) or complex and unconscious (to have worked out relationships that are nearly anthropological in their remoteness from the familiar surfaces).

The ritual aspect of American theatre has been emphasized in some recent discussions about Edward Albee in order to account for his success, which has been especially galling to a number of observers, including a divine, Tom F. Driver, of Union Theological Seminary. He concludes an essay titled "What's the Matter with Edward Albee?" that was published in the *Reporter*, January 2 1964, and reprinted in *American Drama and Its Critics* (1965), as follows:

> This accounts, I believe, for the so-called "involvement" of the audience at *Who's Afraid of Virginia Woolf?* Since the situation and the characters are false, the play provides an occasion for the display of pseudo-emotions: mock anger, mock hatred, mock envy, and finally mock love. These are provided on stage by the actors, with whom the audience enters into complicity. Thus the audience achieves, at no expense to its real emotions, a mock catharsis.
>
> In addition, there is reason to suppose that the

very roughness and the gaucheries that mar Albee's plays contribute to his success. Most of the values that operate in our society are drawn from the bourgeois ideal of domestic harmony, necessary for the smooth functioning of the machine. Yet we know that there are subconscious desires fundamentally in conflict with the harmonious ideal. Albee satisfies at once the ideal and the hidden protest against it. In his badly written plays he jabs away at life with blunt instruments. If his jabbing hit the mark, that would be another matter. But it doesn't, no more than does the child in the nursery when he tears up his toys. That is why Albee is the pet of the audience, this little man who looks as if he dreamed of evil but is actually mild as a dove and wants to be loved. In him America has found its very own playwright. He's a dream.

"Ritual" of one sort or another does seem to characterize the most recent off-Broadway successes and failures of any importance. The ritual aspect of *The Connection*—the formalized waiting—has been remarked on. Another work of The Living Theatre, which originally staged *The Connection* and *The Red Eye of Love*, was *The Brig*, a deadpan, unplotted, theatrically unmodulated depiction of a day in a U.S. Marine stockade for its own prisoners. The work was shattering to the eardrums and the nerves of audiences as the actors performed the fixed, dancelike, rigidly disciplined routines of Marine prisoners, as they woke up in formation, went to wash in formation and called out for orders in loud, mechanical voices, using a prescribed vocabulary.

A number of works are closely related to the highly topical and satirical, frequently improvised sketches prepared for supper and night clubs. Weinstein's *The Red Eye of Love* has been mentioned; he has not yet received the critical appraisal his work calls for (although his play has been published by Grove Press); he continues principally to write sketches for club performances. Mike Nichols, who began his career as an improvising night-club satirist with Elaine May, went on to direct Broadway successes, *Barefoot in the Park, The Odd Couple,* and *Luv,* and the movie version of *Who's Afraid of Virginia Woolf?,* the seriously sensational film *The Graduate,* that shocked with its candid exposure of generational rituals, and the ambiguously black *Catch-22,* in which the ideals of World War II, against the Nazis, were blurred with the aims of the South Vietnamese operations. His controlled spontaneity has seemed to work most effectively in the context of drama acutely sensitive to the power of taboos.

"Happenings" are the theatrical equivalent of anti-representational "action painting" or of the antimusic of John Cage. These productions, which do not follow any scenario or script, are simply set into motion by an idea, the actors responding to one another and to the audience, with lighting and music similarly determined ad lib. But any such successful event, of course, depends on the tension between its unexpectedness and our expectations—in that theatre, at that time. LeRoi Jones's *Dutchman,* perhaps most notably, displays both the virtues and defects of a happening, in its discursive lengthiness and in its seeming spontaneousness. Paradoxically, some dramatic experiments, like those by Lionel Abel or the ensemble performances of *Tom Paine* or *Futz!,* depend on highly formalized activity, however seemingly uncontrived some wilder moments may seem. Kopit's *Dad, Poor Dad,* however jazzed up with balletlike absurdities (Jerome Robbins, the choreographer, directed) and gaglines and gimmicks, was a highy schematized rendition of a classical Oedipal situation.

American drama since the end of World War II has shown bursts of energy suggesting that a renascence is going on similar to the one that followed World War I, and possibly greater. The current equivalents of the Provincetown Players, founded just after World War I, may be found throughout the country, on college campuses, like Yale's Drama School, and at the Washington Theatre Club or Sir Tyrone Guthrie's play-house in Minneapolis, where companies produce both the classics and the work of new playwrights. The Santa Fe Opera Company in New Mexico has pioneered in producing for the first time in the United States avant-garde operatic works whose main emphasis is dramatic, Alban Berg's *Lulu* and Shostakovich's *The Nose*, an "absurd" text based on Gogol and proscribed in the Soviet Union. The Ford Foundation, in an experiment that lasted too short a time to show serious results just yet, sponsored the attachment to theatrical companies throughout the country of novelists and poets so that they might absorb some of the pleasures and crafts of the theatre.

Important, too, in the renascence has been the recent work of a group of critics who are more than merely journalists or merely academicians: Mary McCarthy, Abel, Susan Sontag, Stanley Kauffmann, Brustein, Jack Richardson, Diana Trilling (briefly), Henry Popkin, Gerald Weales; they combine a scholar's width and depth of perspective with the good critic's or philosopher's instinct for rearranging old formulations and suggesting new ones. Troubled by their power through the newspapers and magazines to become accessories in merely financial success or failure, other critics have taken to seeking out noncommercial theatrical endeavors anywhere in New York or in the country, and to attempting essayistic appraisals rather than immediate, deadline-harried reports.

Albee has perhaps built his success on distilling too immediately fashionable essences of the absurd theatre and of pop art, especially in *The American Dream*. (But then the title of this work may well justify any such distillation.) The point of Albee, however, as it was of Tennessee Williams, when he was the theatre's fair-haired young man or of Arthur Miller, or of Clifford Odets (all of whom got *their* lumps when riding high) is that he may be satisfying current and deep American needs that can only be satisfied in the American theatre at this time in his particular way. We may find in the history of the theatre, or in that of any art, that some periods and some peoples have allowed themselves to be satisfied with works that have turned out to have no redeeming aesthetic merit whatsoever, that could be justified and understood by later or different peoples only as sociological or anthropological phenomena. But I think we should pause to consider that some Restoration observers responded to Shakespeare patronizingly, and that it is generally easier to sneer than it is to catch strange idioms and learn and understand new ways. The American theatre probably suffers more from its uniqueness than others because success asserts such a powerfully shaping role in it, and, while Americans cannot live comfortably with success, they cannot live at all without it.

Notes on the New Senecanism
Violence in the American Theatre

The plays of Seneca, Latin tragedies derived largely from Euripides, were marked, as the dictionaries say, by an "accumulation of horrors." Senecan plays were popular in Renaissance Italy, France, and England. Although the blood, lust, and revenge motifs were ultimately subdued or refined, the Senecan form has remained a tempting possibility for every serious dramatist since the seventeenth century if only because of the sensational surface of violence and shock. Its most significant modern manifestation is in very recent drama, principally American, where it has taken on a new vitality and immediacy. The grotesque, Gothic, bizarre, melodramatic in the older Senecanism has become naturalistic, a form of realism.

The Living Theatre, as noted earlier, crystallized many of the qualities of the new Senecanism, producing two works off-Broadway that attained national notoriety, *The Connection* and *The Brig*. The first showed a gathering of dope addicts waiting for the delivery of heroin. The second was a literal, moment-by-moment record of experience in a U. S. Marine prison.

For *The Connection*, the theatre was made virtually part of the stage; the action started in the audience and moved across the footlights; the curtain was never lowered, and members of the audience, according to one report, on occasion expected the characters to come down among them and panhandle to pay for the awaited drug. In his review, Lionel Abel suggested that it might have been especially effective "to announce that anyone seated in the theatre had a right to a shot of 'horse.' Actors could have been stationed in the audience who would respond, and we would have been fascinated by the possibility of being in on the fix too."

The Brig was perhaps one of the loudest plays ever produced. The prisoners screamed all their requests. Among other things, the play was a violent assault against one's usual level of decibel tolerance.

For all of their documentary appearance, perhaps precisely because of it, the two plays tightly observed the simple classical unities. The time was equal to chronological time; the setting remained the same; there was a single action and tone. Yet there were no other qualities of the classical drama, no flawed hero, no peripeteia, no deus ex machina (unless Cowboy, the Negro dressed in white who finally brings the heroin, may be considered as such); the activity in the plays could have started earlier and ended later and might have included any other group of characters doing the same thing. It could have been any collection of addicts we were watching, or any military prison. The Living Theatre might as readily have been called Theatrical Life. Not so irrelevantly as might first seem, the troupe kept running afoul of the police. On one occasion, the newspapers reported, actors were arrested for carrying their performance into the streets, followed by the audience.

What was the point of these works? Both were marked by frequent outbursts of savagery and by a coolness toward excess that, by itself, to use Kenneth Tynan's word, was "shattering." In both works, toilets were prominent in the setting. The language was bluntly direct and obscene. The plays were not simply reaching for *any* sort of candor, but for a candor extreme in its revelation and its potential for offending. They approached a clinical exhibitionism. Lionel Abel suggested that the members of the audience at *The Connection* were actually themselves looking for a fix, to make connection with a meaningful experience, to find some stimulation in the theatre that might carry over into their lives. Robert Brustein in his review suggested that to the extent that the audience got caught up in the action, it was itself "motivated by a voyeuristic interest in freak shows," that to the extent that it believed in the reality of the characters, it was violating "their privacy." Tynan, Brustein, and Abel emphasized the straining honesty of the work and its pointed connections to what we think of as "normal" life.

The acknowledged controlled pretense of Broadway theatre, which is to say of conventional American drama, these plays demonstrated, was no longer capable of provoking the necessary visceral response preliminary to geniune sympathy and catharsis, however skillfully that theatre broke down for the moment any suspension of disbelief. (Not that it didn't try. Miller's *After the Fall* is an exhausting, pleading harangue of the audience for understanding and exculpation by the main character.) The new Senecans are bringing the bear pit into the theatre; unlike Shakespeare they are not *merely* going to compete with bearbaiting and other forms of actual bloodletting. The eye-gouging and limb-amputating in Shakespeare were to be only a small part of the gore. We were to be exposed to psychological as well as physical trauma.

In our time, the commercial Broadway theatre has become too sharply separated from other forms of American mass entertainment. There is an abyss between it and wrestling matches, rodeos, prizefights, nightclub performances, and those multitudinous other events that bring crowds out throughout the country. Road shows that emanate from some New York headquarters resemble older traveling entertainments: *That Was Burlesque*, for example. Because drama is so specifically literary, made up of words arranged in an order, we separate theatrical drama from the drama of life. But there is a continuum between Ugo Betti's *Corruption in the Palace of Justice* and the transcripts of the Congressional hearings involving Frank Costello, the late Senator Joe McCarthy, Senator Dodd, the nomination to Chief Justice of Abe Fortas; between the Philadelphia, Mississippi, lynching of a Negro boy and his two white companions and James Baldwin's *Blues for Mr. Charlie*; between LeRoi Jones's *Dutchman* and *The Slave* and the Newark and Watts riots; between Vietnam and the early American treatment of the Indians.

The phenomenon of "happenings," a little old-fashioned by now if not altogether played out, records the impulse to look in reality itself for theatre. We speak of "making the scene" as though we are indeed walking into and out of a theatrical setting.

Most recent modern drama has returned to the Senecan practice of showing onstage offstage acts of violence. Today, the audience is invited to share in the bloodletting. Gorki's *The Lower Depths* or O'Neill's *The Emperor Jones* aimed at involving the audience atmospherically, expressionistically, rather than literally. Today we become accessories, witnesses.

Curiously, one might argue that the particular violent acts onstage are not significant in and of themselves; they illuminate a more important central action. When Grandma slowly buries herself alive while lying in a beach sandbox, in Albee's play, the *process* of the immolation is the point rather than simply the asphyxiation. In *The American Dream*, the model of young

American manhood occupying the center of the stage in a golden glow, all muscles flexing away simultaneously, talks at length about his physical dismemberment by his parents because of his infantile interest in his sexual parts. Whitney Balliett, writing in the *New Yorker*, remarked on the "forbidding" presence in *The American Dream* of "the butchery and perversion of the Greek theatre." Yet, these were part of one moment only in the panorama of one family's lifelong living out of its American dream, which was the larger event we were asked to witness. The anatomizing of the peculiar yet powerful marital relationship in *Who's Afraid of Virginia Woolf?* offers a prolonged, excessively clinical study of the tortures and horrors of a domesticity held together by suppressed brutalities and masquerades. The play gives us the raw material traditionally antecedent to conventional tragedy while simultaneously proposing a new tragic form. We never see Captain and Mrs. Alving confront (or affront) one another in *Ghosts;* what we see in Ibsen are the ultimate consequences of what we surmise must have been as mutually abrasive and destructive a daily encounter as that between George and Martha. Where George or Martha might end up is not so much the point as where they are right now. Harold Pinter, too, specializes, as in *The Caretaker* or in *A Slight Ache,* in the immediately mysterious, frightening, disgusting emanations of the directly clinical.

For all of their apparent similarities, we should not consider the new Senecan plays as a group. The horror, the shock, the sadism in many is often and in good measure gratuitous, self-contained, not organic to any but the thinnest and most slippery theme. The lunatic gyrations, for example, in Marat/Sade (*The Persecution and Assassination of Marat as Performed by the Inmates of the Asylum of Charenton under the Direction of the Marquis de Sade*) are those of the carnival sideshow, isolated, balletlike ends in themselves, the gestures of animated figures out of the wax museum. On the other hand, we have LeRoi Jones's *The Toilet*, whose very title has the quality of Senecan shock in its immediate offensiveness. But Jones's play also happens to be one of the genuinely touching, nearly sentimental, ones of the modern Senecan repertory. It is, actually, conventionally constructed. The details of the play are loathesome, but in totality it breaks through an instinctive revulsion and engages our sympathy.

The Toilet is especially effective in outraging expectation while disarming our resistance. How are we to have the arms we throw up to shield our vision twisted so painfully behind our backs that we must look at the toilets of our civilization? The new Senecanism may have other intentions and other effects, but it insists, first, on holding an unsparing dialogue with the audience. Pirandello, of course, also put a burden of responsibility on the observer for the action on the stage. He anticipated the current Senecan fashion of mercilessly forcing the onlooker—in *It Is So! (If You Think So)*, for example—to share in the thoughtless lustfulness and then the frustration of the privacy invaders on the stage. Brecht's alienation effect, Artaud's theatre of brutality, absurd drama, also insist that audiences have to be forced to participate in the ceremony of experience in the modern theatre.

We should distinguish as well between the literal expressionism of a playwright like Arnold Wesker and the troubling clinical tone of one like Harold Pinter. The plays of Pinter provide a form of actual documentation of violence and brutality. The texts themselves may be used as evidence. The plays are not *about* violence; they incorporate, include, project violence itself and the tones of violence. In *The Homecoming*, for example, the father ejaculates a mouthful of spit across the stage at another character. In *The Caretaker*, we are subjected to a long monologue by a man who has undergone something like a prefrontal lobotomy. It is true enough that Wesker's plays give us the texture of reality. *The Kitchen* offers a minute-by-minute record of life in the kitchen of a large restaurant, including the jealous outburst by one of the butchers, who breaks a water pipe with a cleaver. But all of this is not only familiar but classifiable; it corroborates our established knowledge of such matters. There is no attempt to violate or transcend the familiar. The territory has been mapped for us many times before.

Pinter, by contrast, is compelling us to observe or, at least, to sense new areas, to participate in disquieting modern rituals, whose nature we sometimes barely discern, let alone understand. *The Homecoming* is one of the blackest comedies since *Measure for Measure.* The laughter it provokes is that of the autonomic nervous system, the uncomfortable, uncontrolled jerk of the hiccup. We are outraged, baffled, teased, amused, tickled, insulted. In Pinter, in short, the spittle that hurls across the stage may be real and shocking, but what hurts is its source of animal hate and animal action. In Wesker, the water that spurts from the broken pipe is only that and can only wet us. We can dry off water easily enough with a towel; we cannot so easily expunge the shock of case history.

We may find early manifestations of the new Senecanism in some of the more intense scenes in Eugene O'Neill (*Desire under the Elms*, or *Mourning Becomes Electra*, which derive more from Seneca's adaptations of Greek originals than from the originals themselves) or in Federico García Lorca (*Blood Wedding, Yerma, The House of Bernarda Alba*), and perhaps in some of the plays of social protest in the thirties, although the Senecan moralizing was perhaps stronger there than any explicit Senecan violence.

Anger is an important informing quality of the new

Senecanism, and the angry young playwrights of England immediately after World War II certainly approached forms of violence that were later to become the very substance of the drama. John Osborne's *Look Back in Anger*, *The Entertainer*, and *Inadmissible Evidence* made deliberate efforts to involve the audience in the total dramatic experience. In *Inadmissible Evidence*, the leading character keeps his sense of being alive through a willed nastiness. "I hate, I insult, therefore I live." The autobiographical hints in *The Hotel in Amsterdam* offer a vague gesture of apology through self-pity as they simultaneously suggest the drift from mindless anger to childish, self-indulgent absurdity.

The theatre of violence must make the stage a part of life and find in life its own various stages. In Genet's *The Blacks*, Archibald, the master of ceremonies, directly confronts a member of the audience, invites him into the action and viciously rejects him, offers him a stick used in a stage ritual, then violently takes it back and cracks it in half. We are not different mortally from the actors on the stage, nor they from us; what happens there happens here; as we surround the action in an arena stage, it surrounds us. (Negroes at performances of *The Blacks* muttered revivallike calls of approval at the nightly ritual murder of a white woman.) In Albee's *Tiny Alice*, the sickness on stage communicates in waves outward, envelops us. As the miniature replica of the house on stage reproduces the ugly and strange action around it, so the microcosm of the actual stage, we sense with nausea, may be reproducing the action of the larger, total house we are in, orchestra, balcony, lobby, street, city, nation, the whole macrocosm.

One of the most shocking Senecan plays of recent times presents persons as grotesque dolls. In *Motel*, by Jean-Claude van Itallie, a male and female manikin enter a motel room to the accompaniment of the recorded monologue of the papier-mâché lady motel manager. They copulate, draw dirty pictures on the mirror, then tear everything apart, including the motel manager, dismembering her totally, including her head covered with hair rollers. Here, too, the toilet is important. It "flushes of its own accord," the recording assures the manikins. "All you've got to do is get off. Pardon my mentioning it, but you'll have to go far before you see a thing like that on this route." And indeed the sound of the flushing can be heard at appropriate intervals. The toilet seat itself is ripped off in the course of the vandalism.

Robert Brustein, in his review of the play, later published as the introduction to *America Hurrah*, the trilogy, speaks of *Motel* as

> based on a metaphor so powerful that it may well become the objective correlative of the Johnson age. . . . Vladimir Nabokov effectively used motel culture, in *Lolita*, as an image of the sordidness and taste-lessness in the depths of our land; Mr. van Itallie uses it as an image of our violence, our insanity, our need to defile.
>
> He has, in short, discovered the deepest poetic function of the theatre which is . . . to invent metaphors which can poignantly suggest a nation's nightmares and afflictions.

That the new Senecanism reflects some deep-seated and even popular need of our time may be demonstrated even more vividly through Michael McClure's *The Beard*, an extended theatrical metaphor, to use Brustein's expression, about two American culture heroes from widely separated periods and in entirely different contexts—Billy the Kid, the young New Mexican killer of the nineteenth century, and Jean Harlow, the quintessential and reputedly sexually insatiable movie star of our own century. *The Beard* may be described, before anything else, as self-destructive by its own nature, like those pieces of mechanized sculpture by Jean Tinguely, which operated slowly toward their own extinction.

The play is of such a character, in vocabulary and climax (the only significant action comes at the end; all else is a nearly static, repetitive dialogue although there is some movement by the two principles, and at one point Billy the Kid tears some of Jean Harlow's clothes), as to demand almost immediate closing down by the authorities of whatever establishment in whose midst it may be performed. It provokes an immediate cathartic reaction to itself, overflowing with the sorts of obscenities and exchanges, blunt, monosyllabically Anglo-Saxon, simple and simpleminded, the vocabulary of toilet-wall graffiti, which are normal idiom only in the depths or on the fringes of our familiar, polite society. It is repetitious in a compulsive, palimpsestic manner; the underlayers are images of the top surface of shallowness and constricted mindlessness, the result of the public and long-sustained nurturing of the childish selfishness of our culture heroes. Our newspaper stars become reduced to puppets who destroy themselves by believing in themselves. The final scene of *The Beard* (a title that irreverently suggests not only the moustache on the Mona Lisa but the female pubic hair) is explicitly sexual, involving cunnilingus, an act declared by statute to be illegal in a number of states.

Yet the work is obviously metaphorical and can hardly be described by any usual theatregoer as erotic—any more than those fornicating manikins in *Motel* are erotic. The monotonous, near-moronic, ritualistic, childishly chantlike exchanges between Billy the Kid and Jean Harlow in their tinsel heaven have nothing to do with any recognizable, documentary reality. The intensity of their sustained mutual insulting of and swearing at each other is reminiscent only of other metaphorical situations, like those in *Waiting for Godot* or in *No Exit*. It is extravagantly overresponsive to surface, perhaps a form of self-defense, to allow proper anger or strained outrage to blur the horror, the abominable extremity of their fate, of what consciousness must be like in eternity for the doll-like creatures who have greatness thrust upon them by a rotten culture.

The police, the uniformed, immediately identifiable representatives of the establishment, will have nothing to do with Coleridge's injunctions about suspending disbelief. They believe, they believe. They act on what they see and hear, on the evidence, on what can be recorded on tape or on film. They do not look for symbol. They purge society of what is clearly antisocial or extrasocial; this is their role, and their playing of it is a key to what is literal, to the nitty-gritty awareness that must precede any larger vision. In their immediate self-purgative effectiveness, in their insistence that they be taken in the first place literally, that they be closed down as a measure of their success, works like *The Beard* must be evaluated by objective, quantitative standards: how fast before the fuzz move in to arrest actors and audience? Lenny Bruce's performances met similar criteria.

Saved, a British play by Edward Bond, was refused "a license for public performance . . . as it stands," an introductory note to the published text tells us. The situation which made the play offensive, causing some members of the private audience to rush out of the theatre vomiting, was the brutal pummeling and squashing to death of an infant in its carriage by a group of British hoodlums. Actually in the context of the work, the murder of the baby is, as in so many of the other modern plays incorporating violence, on the edge of the central action, which has to do with the attempt of the central character, Len, to keep himself attached to a family arrangement. Like the stomping to death of the father in another British play, *Entertaining Mr. Sloane*, by Joe Orton, the onstage murder is not the central situation. In Orton's play a gangsterish brother and a somewhat addled sister are in competition for the affections of a delinquent young man who has moved into the household as a boarder.

"Clearly the stoning to death of a baby in a London park is a typical English understatement," Bond says in his preface to the published play. "Compared to the 'strategic' bombing of German towns it is a negligible atrocity, compared to the cultural and emotional deprivation of most of our children its consequences are insignificant." If the play horrifies us all that much, the proposition seems to be, it is because we are not sufficiently horrified, if at all, by the fate of children in Mississippi, Biafra, India, Mexico.

The new Senecanism has a comic mode as well as tragic and melodramatic ones. The most familiar manifestation of the comic mode is in the black-humor dramatic monologues of stand-up comedians like Mort Sahl, Bob Newhart, Jonathan Winters, the Smothers Brothers, Jack E. Leonard, Don Rickles, and, most particularly, the late Lenny Bruce.

In drama specifically, the comic mode may be found in such plays as *The Red Eye of Love*, by Arnold Weinstein, already referred to, and *Oh Dad, Poor Dad, Mama's Hung You in the Closet and I'm Feeling So Sad*, by Arthur L. Kopit. Kopit takes the hackneyed Oedipal situation as the basis for a sustained and sometimes skittish study of the malignant influence of a domineering mother on her grown son. Among other props, the play contains a piranha, which at one point almost bites off the hand of a bellboy in a hotel; a flesh-eating plant; and the body of the late Dad, whom mother has killed, which she keeps in her funeral bedroom. The corpse falls onto the bed where a baby-sitter is seducing the son, causing a somewhat violent overreaction: he strangles the girl.

Other forms of the Senecan comic mode are the "put-on" and certain types of camp. A number of *off*-off Broadway productions illustrate the fashion; perhaps the most characteristic was *Gorilla Queen*, by Ronald Tavel. This was an extended parody of American jungle movies of the thirties and forties. Like an Olsen and Johnson production, the play poured over the footlights and into the lobby, involving the audience, before, during, and after the actual stage business, which included masturbating monkeys, a human sacrifice, and bestiality (in the specific legal sense). The play *Futz!* by Rochelle Owens, is about a man in love with a pig— a sow, that is, not a boar—with which he has intercourse. In *Medea*, a modern adaptation by H. M. Koutoukas, the jilted mother stuffs her children into public washing machines, where they are mangled to death. Some of these plays go to various extremes of physical assault to shock audiences into attention. In *La Turista*, by Sam Shepard, the dialogue consists of the simultaneous shouting at each other by the two principals. The director of one troupe was quoted: "The playwright [we sponsor] has complete freedom to offend and to disgust our audiences."

Black or sick comedy, so popular in our own age, has its roots and analogues in the works of Aristophanes, Molière, Jonathan Swift, Mark Twain, and in gallows humor generally. The motivating dynamic of *Lysistrata* is nothing less than war itself. Shaw's "comedies" about such figures as Mrs. Warren, the chairlady of the board of an international cartel of brothels, and about Andrew Undershaft, a munitions maker, have a black cast. Senecan comedy, however, has not yet been comfortably, authentically assimilated, I think, to the modern theatre, although it may well turn out to be the natural American idiom for modern tragedy. (See the next chapter.) Black comedy in the theatre must break out from traditional forms and find or adapt unexpected and new ones. *The Red Eye of Love* was greeted by dismay and anger by some critics since it seemed so offhand, frivolous, and scarcely "dramatic" in the expected usual Broadway sense of the word. The fact that the play was sensitively informed by an awareness of early slapstick movies, that it brilliantly incorporated vaudeville and burlesque-house routines, that it adapted some of the more successful devices of nightclub comedians, all of this went unnoticed by critics looking for more conventional structure and subject matter. Yet Weinstein's play prepared the way for Kopit's *Indians*, for *Hair*, and for *Motel*.

How can we characterize some of the differences among the Senecan plays that have come to us from France, England, Germany, as well as from the United States? The intermingling of various national trends in drama has been so substantial in recent years, with plays being made into films so very soon after stage production, and with the growing art of translation, that it may be pointless, if temptingly easy, to talk about lingering specific national qualities. Yet British black drama, for example, may be read as more personal, more focused on particular individuals and particular situations, as in *Look Back in Anger*, *A Taste of Honey*, *Serjeant Musgrave's Dance*, *Saved*, *Entertaining Mr. Sloane*, *The Hotel in Amsterdam*, or *Joe Egg*. In this respect at least they differ from the larger "metaphorical" ambitions of American black writers, who work by generalization and allegory: *Motel*, *The Red Eye of Love*, *Indians*, *Futz!*, or the plays satirizing, say, the television industry or jungle movies or Madison Avenue. Where Dostoyevsky, with his accounts of personal hells, may be said to energize British Senecan drama, Kafka with his allegories provides sources for American. Pirandello seems the inspiration for France. French Senecan plays, most particularly Genet's *The Blacks* or *The Balcony* but also works like Anouilh's *Antigone* or Ionesco's repertory, are often more concerned with technique, with establishing devices which in themselves would say something to us about subject: the fact, for example, that Genet (in *The Maids* and in *The Screens*) endlessly explores some of the relations between illusion and reality as a means of understanding reality. Ritual, repetition, becomes abstracted from individual, whimsical acts that may also have been repeated often. Bertolt Brecht or Peter Weiss, in their attempts at an epic sweep, suggest something of the classical Germanic panoramic vision, with which we have become familiar in the works of Thomas Mann or of Beethoven.

Art does more than reflect or record reality. Art gives us ways of understanding reality, of assimilating it to some hoped-for order and informed apprehension that may provide whatever comfort there may be of strong feeling or of settled understanding, or, ideally, ultimately of both. In an affluent society, we can buy not only forms of happiness but also the means to insulate ourselves from feeling or thinking altogether if we find that the reach for pleasure or for understanding runs any risk of any pain. All art must shock *le bourgeois*, which is to say the middle-class establishment, in the first place, one way or another, before it goes on to do other things, including the offering of pleasure. Picasso's *Guernica*, as horrible as it is carefully ordered, if it satisfies in any aesthetic way at all does so because of its truthfulness as well as its excess. Senseless, unmotivated, casual, frivolous, profitable, self-indulgent brutality, murder, torture in the world at large often do not penetrate our usual defenses against outrage because they are unstructured, inorganic, accidental; organized forms of man's inhumanity to man, like concentration camps, atomic explosions in populated areas, mass starvation, organized denial of education, war itself, we must exclude altogether as threats to our esteem and psychic well-being, for they are sanctioned by society and thus, ultimately, necessarily by ourselves. It is possible for the serious playwright today to apply Senecan intentions in small, realistic situations (or in large but metaphorical ones) more readily than to do so in the dimensions called for by concentration camps, apartheid, Latin American dictatorships, the Vietnam and African confusions. But always the immensity of the larger world looms over the stage; we focus on the microscopic disordered cell, for we sense that it is finally organically linked to the larger cancer.

Drama in any age has a social dynamic. Some of our leading Senecans are or have been activists in violent affairs, Jean Genet, LeRoi Jones, Joe Orton, Norman Mailer. The gulf between the ideal and the real, between the best for man and the worst, is visibly getting wider. Simultaneously, we are forced to become more aware of that gulf. It was in South Africa, the only country in the modern world where a class of human beings are by law defined to lack even minimal human capacities or needs, that the first successful heart transplant was sustained. Progress in the Western world to minimize pain and discomfort of every sort has been enormous, an achievement that makes our failure all the more dismal to ease everywhere poverty, illiteracy, human disfranchisement of any kind. Our affluent Western society, to labor the point, has marvelously learned to anesthetize itself. It has not learned altogether, not yet anyhow, to kid itself about all the abominations. However reluctantly, someone is paying attention to the new

Senecans; we can't imprison every Lenny Bruce or LeRoi Jones, and we cannot always defend ourselves by charging with sickness all the writers who speak to us disturbingly. The Dostoyevskys and the Jonathan Swifts will be heard in any age.

8

Toward an American Tragedy

Will we ever have the great American novel? Can there be a true American tragedy? Such questions are not merely academic, stimuli for idle critical speculation. We know that a literary form (or other art form) can be a guide to the character of an age or of a people. Whatever the answer may be for the novel, for tragedy any attempt at an answer holds out the possibility of defining and understanding what is quintessentially American today. Tragedy, even an effort toward tragedy, provides a crystallization of the American character not readily available in other forms of evidence. Without raising any larger aesthetic issue, we may say for the moment that literary art achieves its most distilled character in tragedy if only for the reasons Stephen Dedalus formulated so simplistically: the drama, speaking for itself and through itself, excluding the narrator, or, rather, deifying him into a detached, remote, objective observer, must come closer than the lyric or epic, poetry or fiction, to presenting the external world as it is in something close to its total complexity. Further, without proposing any new poetics, we may assume that the only sort of serious drama we can have is a form of tragedy.

The fact of the matter is, plainly, that serious American dramatists have strained more ambitiously to work in tragedy than in any other form. O'Neill's efforts, while the most prodigious in fulfillment, were not aimed primarily at producing an *American* tragedy, however, but a universal one. I do not mean to be simply paradoxical here, for clearly such works as *Desire under the Elms* and *Long Day's Journey into Night* are unmistakably "American" in their record of struggle to work out a means of dignified survival against a hostile earth, almost literally so in the New England landscape of *Desire,* and certainly metaphorically so in *Long Day's Journey.* What makes O'Neill finally "less" American is the same thing that makes Shakespeare "less" British: their success in transcending the particular and immediate while simultaneously recording and celebrating it. O'Neill's American character, then, depends on what has finally become monumental and universally recognizable and, most significantly, no longer just local and possibly transitional. Of course, as the American writer ultimately succeeds in writing an *American* tragedy, he also fails, for the work rises to another class, that of universal tragedy. But we have had few such grand failures.

The attempt to record the dynamic nature of the American setting, that very changing scene which it becomes almost dangerous to fix in any moment lest it be thereby falsified, characterizes the technique of such social dramatists as Odets, Hellman, Miller, and Williams. But in terms of the Joycean distinction among the epic, lyric, and dramatic, these are more epic writers than dramatic ones. They control the activity of their text; one way or another they comment on the action and do not often allow it to achieve its own identity and integrity. They are concerned with "epic" subjects, the transition from feudalism to capitalism in the South, the conflict between classes or social types, the effects in human terms of great economic forces. Their plays have been noble efforts at serious drama, but they add up finally only to forms of history rather than of poetry, certainly not of tragedy in any archetypal sense of that word.

Perhaps the very straining for an appearance of greatness has kept American drama from achieving that awe and mystery inherent in the ordinary which shock us into knowledge. American playwrights have tried to fit their efforts into large and familiar classical frames, either into the well-made Ibsenesque structure or into the Shakespearean mold, both much too anachronistically inappropriate for contemporary content. *West Side Story*, for example, for all of its innovative success, fails finally to evoke the tragic density even of its original, *Romeo and Juliet*. While we might have expected that the musical would have a larger dimension than the original Shakespearean model, since the lovers come not from feuding families but from opposing social groups, the conflict becomes blurred by being set in two contexts, the personal and the social. It is not the power of the irrational and whimsical which shapes events but of definable and, therefore, presumably controllable arrangements in society. Curiously, the genuine tragic territory of *West Side Story* may be found not in the doomed love of the two young people but in the suggestion of the generational hostility between the young gangs and the police establishment, a dim echo of Mercutio's adolescent hotheadedness as opposed to the sobriety of the family organizations. (The Zeffirelli film emphasizes this conflict between the young and the old.)

The weight of the evidence, nevertheless, is clear that any serious American drama must find its valid subject matter and its proper dynamic in the relation of an individual to a social milieu. Tragedy is, after all and before all, "political": Oedipus was the king and savior of his country: that political fact defines his tragedy as a son and husband; Hamlet committed himself to determine what was rotten in the state of Denmark, on the occasion of the death of his father, the king, and, in spite of himself, to set the time right politically; Chekhov's aristocrats, Ibsen's middle-class heroes and heroines, Strindberg's Miss Julie and the captain, were all living on the infirm soil of societies in transition. The problem, of course, is to isolate the particular political territory of a play and then to determine the seriousness and accuracy of the politics.

We know all too well that those American plays about which we have held pietistic estimates of their seriousness have all been energized by a "profound social awareness," from Hellman's to Miller's: the question is how "social" and how "aware," let alone how "profound." Doctrinaire, party-line oversimplification, shrill Messianic dedication, alone do not produce valid or even plausible results. It is the writer's unmediated relation to his material that determines the effectiveness of the finished work, not his relation to an idea about the material (although, of course, such a preliminary commitment may well affect the inner content and outer look of the final work). To the extent that American writers of serious drama were able to achieve, in spite of themselves sometimes, a sense of the American scene that was independent of some predetermined, intended solemnity of thought, were they able to produce the forms, tones, and surfaces of tragedy. The intention to record "landscape" in Hellman and in Odets, for example, hints at the later American adaptation of the Brechtian theatre of impersonal epic width, of a documentary diminution of individual heroes, the abstracted distortion of mysterious movements across deep and spreading landscapes.

Explorations in technique were in significant measure aspects of the movement toward an American tragedy. The panoramic sweep of the Federal Theatre's Living

Newspaper, for example, concentrated not on personages but on nonheroic persons and the situations in which they were enmeshed. It was the documentary texture that made *One Third of a Nation* more than a sentimental, poignant, and limited newspaper feature. The expressionistic plays of Elmer Rice were efforts at devising an air of tragedy; his *Street Scene,* while more conventional, records an American urban community in something of an epic operatic texture (like Lillian Hellman's *The Little Foxes, Street Scene* was rendered into a form of serious musical drama). The total tragic effect calls for more than the mere clashing of ignorant armies on the plains of Troy observed from a distant height. We need to see the delicately delineated figures of individual Greeks and Trojans, human beings with whom we feel some identity of emotional and moral commitment. We need, above all, to have created for us some sense of an important and large American environment: that of war, of politics, of business, of race relations, of scientific change. It is curious that we have not had any serious effort to derive drama from the careers of, say, an Eisenhower or a MacArthur, giant figures moving through mighty events, but we have had, almost by contrast, smaller and more modest records like *Command Decision,* in which a solemn effort was made to derive serious drama from the temptation to succumb to the reductive moral simplicity so readily available in any high command. The problems of a general having to send a thousand planes to bomb a factory, are, obviously, for all the possible casualties, much easier to pose, discuss, and dramatize than those of a commander-in-chief having to decide on dropping an atom bomb on a city. No American dramatist has yet taken up the challenge offered in the works of historians and journalists about the background of the decisions to pinpoint Hiroshima and Nagasaki, or of

Roosevelt's relation to the German concentration camps, or of the public tragedy of Oppenheimer.

On a smaller scale, of course, we have had small gestures at serious drama in anatomizing the personal frictions and dilemmas of the business world, in plays like *Point of No Return*, about bank or corporation vice-presidents and other such functionaries, again not about the top figures of the automobile or of the steel or of the mining industry, the Fords, the Knudsens, the Fricks, the Mellons, the Rockefellers. Our political plays have been either topical comedies, like *The State of the Union* or *The Best Man*, or simpleminded exercises in dishonest rhetoric, like *Inherit the Wind*, the Clarence Darrow–William Jennings Bryan opposition on the occasion of the Scopes trial, a possibility that in its very naming suggests one of the tragic oppositions in Amerian life, that between compulsive, intense, provincial ignorance and dedicated, modest, relaxed, urbane enlightenment.

We have found it difficult to distill tragedy from the career even of an Abraham Lincoln, confining ourselves, in what is probably the best play about that president, to his youth, *Abe Lincoln in Illinois*, which has hovering over it, of course, the cloud of the later tragedy. The attempt to manufacture serious drama from Franklin D. Roosevelt's attack of polio suggests the constriction of the American dramatic imagination, in *Sunrise at Campobello*, as though tragedy can be made simply from the stolidly researched presentation of a sad affliction. The tragedy of Woodrow Wilson's failure, while part of the historical record, has not been transmuted into literary art. We have had, thankfully, considering the previous failures, no similar efforts with the Kennedy brothers.

Perhaps it is a particular setting itself, inevitably, sharply illuminated, shaded infinitely by the whimsy and

improvisation of reality, that may provide an environment at least for tragedy. The world of a drug addict,
understood to be imposed on our larger world, rooted in
it, organically derived from it, opens at least one room
in which to set some tragic figures in motion: surely we
cannot deny the tragic import of Jack Gelber's *The
Connection*, the connection it may make with our own
emptily obsessed lives. Our homogenized motel culture,
our sickeningly trivialized sexual consciousness, suggest
another horror chamber, as in Jean-Claude van Itallie's
Motel. Our worse than dehumanized military penal
system, distilling everything inhumanly uncivilized about
American penal systems in general, is another context,
as in Kenneth Brown's *The Brig*. Our new awareness of
the various irrational domains of the domestic, barely
hinted at in George Kelly and O'Neill, has inspired some
of the grotesqueries of Edward Albee. Yet all of these
remain, finally, either too personal, too microcosmically
private, or too impersonal, too much an arbitrary and
limited record, with too narrowly focused a perspective,
to approach the terror of Yeats's vision, that of the
rough beast dragging itself toward some terrible revelation, commenting by its own presence on the time and
on the people living under its shadow.

Tragedy, in any age in any environment, has had a
metaphorical, a symbolic intention. Shakespeare's histories, when they become more than political presen-
tations, as in *Richard II* or *Richard III*, approach tragedy
by virtue of the heroes' assuming other than biographical
proportions. In our own time, of course, Arthur Miller
in attempting to write the tragedy of a common man
identifies him as "a salesman," names him "low man,"
does not provide any specific information about his
product, in short, attempts to enlarge his significance,
inflating him so that we are no longer concerned only
with a specific defined person but with an idea. We may

certainly look for any emerging American tragic hero
in a mythical figure who derives from a historic one.
The figure, it would seem, should simultaneously combine the idea and the record of some national hero, a
Lindbergh or a Frank Lloyd Wright, a gangster (as in
the film *Bonnie and Clyde*), a charismatic president, a
business magnate, a railroad baron, a scientist, a soldier,
an Indian scout, a poet, a popular singer, a nightclub
comedian, a Hollywood star, a circus performer, a figure,
in short, who in one or another particularized manifestation has commanded the largest American concern
and imagination in an enterprise no one can fail to
recognize as ultimately important to him in some
visceral or intellectual way. The depth, the continuity,
the moral value establishing that importance will provide
the necessary "universality."

The Germans have developed the documentary epic
as one means for moving toward modern tragedy. *In the
Matter of J. Robert Oppenheimer* is a distilled editing
of the enormous investigation conducted to determine
whether or not Dr. Oppenheimer's security clearance
should be continued in his work on theoretical atomic
physics. The tragic issues are sharply stated, stripped of
the normal verbiage of hearings; characters emerge with
surprising sharpness, considering their very brief appearance on the witness stand; and the general coolness
and politeness of the record adds an ironic dimension to
the lurking emotion and horror that the hearing necessarily evokes: the terrible agony of the scientists involved
in preparing a political event which some of them could
scarcely, then or now, embrace with mindful understanding. Yet the work does not assume the final proportions of tragedy, not least because the events are, in
their broad outlines, so familiar to us, the history is
literally presented, in the stiff and formal movements of
an administrative hearing, no effort is made to transcend

the documentary and realistic by means of any of the usual theatrical or literary devices of tragedy: chorus, poetry, or soliloquy, not to speak of music, dance, or lighting. That is, the reader must finally bring his own sense of what tragedy might be in the modern world to the evidence offered us in the production, or by the bare text in the reading. Indeed, given the time and the patience, a greater sense of tragedy might emerge in the course of reading the entire trial record itself. The play serves merely to remind us of the insistent presence of this record. We must acknowledge that the tragedy is there on the agenda someday to be taken up properly.

A similar comment might be made about Rolf Hochhuth's play *The Deputy*, which is a much more fictionalized, if not entirely imagined, presentation of the pope's involvement with the Nazi extermination of the Jews. *The Diary of Anne Frank* was a most moving but finally sentimental rather than tragic rendering of a young girl's response to a particular event. Again, the full sense of tragedy emanating from the play was provided by the spectator or reader himself, as he himself made the larger, the social, the philosophical connections with the idea of Auschwitz.

It was Bertolt Brecht who, more than any other dramatist, sensed and satisfied the need to develop new forms, new idioms, to present tragedy on the modern stage. Brecht worked with practical, theatrical possibilities to present tragedy of a modern character to a modern audience. His relationship to Shaw, who confronted similar problems and resolved them in his own unique way, has been remarked on. Surely *Saint Joan* is among the first "modern" tragedies in form, in its casual disregard of conventional realism and historical accuracy. Shaw's awareness of the perspective of imagination, of the power of an imagined environment to persuade and move, is present in Brecht: the possibilities implicit in sheer inventiveness, in the landscapes of the idea of a stockyard, of a Chicago, of a jungle, of a war. Chronological time, realistic setting, natural dialogue, biographical accuracy, all of these become irrelevant, not necessarily to be discarded but to be subordinated to the achievement of a greater reality, the sense of tragedy in *Saint Joan of the Stockyards* or in *The Good Woman of Setzuan* or in *Galileo*.

In the efforts of a number of young American dramatists, toward the end of the sixties, we may dimly see forms emerging of an American tragedy incorporating Brechtian elements. Discarding highbrow and classical devices, abandoning altogether the forms and idioms of the commercial theatre, these writers have turned to the most familiar, the most available American vocabularies of mass entertainment. Vaudeville turns, slapstick encounters, quickly dissolving cinematic scenes, minstrelshow banter, rodeolike explosive violence, the absurdly reduced bad guy–good guy conflict of television wrestling matches, the bang-bang of westerns and of gangster movies, the enormous advertising dummies of Las Vegas nightclubs and of roadside hamburger stands anywhere, balloons, fireworks, toilet-wall graffiti, that entire Coney Island of the American cotton-candy, campy countryside some of us have for so long excluded from our blinkered vision, have been assimilated into the latest drama: Albee's *The American Dream* and *The Zoo Story*, LeRoi Jones's *Dutchman* and *The Toilet*, van Itallie's *Motel*, Arnold Weinstein's *The Red Eye of Love*, Kopit's *Dad, Poor Dad*, Rochelle Owens's *Futz!*, and such musicals as *Hair*, *Viet Rock*, and *Your Own Thing*.

Arthur Kopit's *Indians* suggests the form, the intention, and the dimension that American drama might have to assume to achieve that identity and integrity we expect of tragedy. Since it is, clearly, an *attempt*, that is, more than an experiment but less than an achievement, it is necessary to speak of it in terms of potential. The play takes the form of a series of vaudeville turns, separate scenes, each with a curious self-sufficiency, the whole finally casting a tone reflectively back on each. The first appearance of Buffalo Bill is on a huge sculpted horse carried by a group of cowboys and Indians, with a great deal of shooting, shouting, and flag-waving: the soldier on horseback transferred from the main squares of small-town America. We see the garish opening parade against a huge advertising poster of Buffalo Bill's Wild West Show. Transitions between scenes are marked by quick slapstick pantomimes, like the one in which an Indian catches in his mouth bullets shot across stage by a cowboy, spitting each bullet into a tin can, the final bullet apparently knocking out all his teeth since there is a rattle into the can as he empties his mouth. Other scenes move from a poker game in a saloon to a formal hearing of the Indian grievances against the government, presided over by three government functionaries made up in newspaper blacks and whites contrasting with the literally, vividly red Indians. (I describe the original London production; some changes were made for Washington and New York presentation.)

Buffalo Bill is the sardonic hero of the work. The Indians expect that he will see justice done to their cause. He himself expects this. Yet caught in the opposition between the government, exemplified by a clownish Uncle Sam president in red, white, and blue long underwear, and the solemn, quietly dignified yet baffled Indians, he cannot implement his good intentions. He can only make gestures in the real world which lies between the excess of dignity of the victimized Indian and the show-biz buffoonery of vicious political caricature applied to the bad guys of the government. He does not know how or why he has been so caught;

he is desperate in his huge puzzlement; at no point until the final scene does he display any insight, not even that of rationalization. His double-talk, his ambivalent, frustrated good intentions—"good" for his government, "good" for the red men—do not show the leavening of any kind of understanding until his fumbling, emotional apology in the final scene, in which, in the attempt to justify himself, he shows the artifacts, the dolls, the shabby workhouse doodads the Indians have been reduced to producing to make a motion toward survival.

The tragedy is not only about an individual, of course, but about a nation. And it is not only about the United States, but about any colonial power. The Indians of the title could be East Indians or Africans. The confused intentions of Buffalo Bill, a civilian involved with military and government administration, is akin to the problems of a civilian American president, a civilian British prime minister, a civilian French president, a civilian Belgian king, who similarly must deal with minority peoples, or colonial peoples, under the combined pressures of history, individual selfishness and whimsicality, the public need for circuses, the indifference of affluence and casual greed, the official fumbling to do right of government agencies: all the sad and agonizing gestures we have become so familiar with in historical events, like the Vietnam or Algerian wars, or the British relationship to Ireland, India, Israel, and the African colonies; or the Belgian occupation of the Congo.

The play is, on first look, simply outrageously anti-American, lampooning the president and the presidency, the flag, the national anthem, and individual heroes. Yet throughout the offensive activities in which hoodlumism, self-indulgence, depravity are vividly and explicitly depicted (an ugly physical encounter between a madam and a dirty, bearded cowboy takes place center stage), Buffalo Bill retains his dignity and an aloof confidence in a happy ending, that faith of the earnest Christian, while it is clear to him and to everyone else that his best intentions are being perverted and ridiculed. This is the tragedy of persons caught up in events, trying to do things that are great and good not only because of the numbers of persons involved but by virtue of the principle infusing and guiding the events. Buffalo Bill emerges not only as the respected and expected savior of the noble red man, who is always depicted in the tableau-like figures of martyrdom, dioramas in a museum, but also as the popular folk hero of the American public. He has a part both in a sad history and in a cheap cartoon strip. His compromises with his own dignity, his subjection of the Indian chiefs who have joined his troop to staged indignities, his confused role as an intermediary between the heartlessly blundering Washington investigators and the patiently suffering Indians make the tragedy which destroys him.

The point here is not the personal and specific disappointment and failure of Mr. William Cody, great as these were, but the panoramic disaster of one American culture hero trying under the pressures of Olympian forces to act heroically. These forces are dedicated, like so many of the original Olympian impulses, to the whimsical, shallow, unprincipled destruction of mere mortals.

Buffalo Bill moves in the two opposing worlds of the simple, sketchily noble primitivism of the Indians (who make set speeches clearly derived from historical records) and that of the stylized western saloon or sideshow made known to us in cowboy movies, television series, and bouncy musical spectaculars like *Annie Get Your Gun*. (*Indians* seems at moments almost a raw, college-produced parody of the Irving Berlin work.) Buffalo Bill has two reputations to live up to, the historical one and the one contrived by talent agents and fellow entertainers. Kopit very deliberately uses our television familiarity with the world of Matt Dillon, all those scenes in saloons where the men play poker, get drunk, fight, break furniture, draw fast, flirt with the ladies of the establishment, to expose that very real, lurking, trigger-sudden terror of rape and casual brutality that one must expect to find in frontier towns, in the callous world of juvenile delinquents, of gangs, of any jungle: the characters all derive from the American entertainment mythology of the West: Bat Masterson, Doc Holliday, Billy the Kid, the Dalton Brothers, and some of their famous lady friends.

Any American tragedy has to acknowledge the quality of American life in the total universe of history, past and present, real and manufactured, actual, possible, and probable. This is that deepest social setting essential to tragedy. We must find also heroes who can function in this setting, heroes whose character and carriage are determined by the social context as well as by their own deepest intentions: only the exact and terrible combination of Thebes in desolation and Oedipus on the make can produce the critical mass of tragedy. As an American tragedy develops, it will surely combine the sense of awful, hard immediacy we find in works like LeRoi Jones's *Toilet* and *Dutchman* with the enormous metaphorical import of others like van Itallie's *Motel* and Rochelle Owens's *Futz!* and Kopit's *Indians*.

Selected Bibliography

Plays by Individual Authors

Albee, Edward. *The American Dream: A Play*. New York: Coward-McCann, 1961.

——. *Who's Afraid of Virginia Woolf?: A Play*. New York: Atheneum, 1962.

Anderson, Maxwell. *Winterset: A Play in Three Acts*. Washington: Anderson House, 1937.

Arent, Arthur. "One-Third of a Nation." *Drama in Our Time*. Ed. Munjon M. Nagelberg. New York: Harcourt, Brace, 1948.

Baldwin, James. *Blues for Mr. Charlie: A Play*. New York: Dial Press, 1964.

Behrman, Samuel N. *Four Plays: The Second Man, Biography, Rain from Heaven, End of Summer*. New York: Random House, 1955.

Blitzstein, Marc. "The Cradle Will Rock." *The Best Short Plays of the Social Theatre*. Ed. William Kozlenko. New York: Random House, 1939.

Brown, Kenneth H. *The Brig: A Concept for Theatre or Film*. New York: Hill and Wang, 1965.

Eliot, T. S. *The Complete Poems and Plays*. New York: Harcourt, Brace & World, Inc., 1962.

Gelber, Jack. *The Connection: A Play*. New York: Grove Press, 1960.

Gibson, William. *The Seesaw Log: A Chronicle of the Stage Production, with Text of "Two for the Seesaw."* New York: Knopf, 1959.

Haines, William W. *Command Decision: A Play*. New York: Random House, 1948.

Hansberry, Lorraine. *A Raisin in the Sun, The Sign in Sidney Brustein's Window, The 101 "Final" Performances of Sidney Brustein*. New York: New American Library, 1966.

Hellman, Lillian. *Four Plays: The Children's Hour, Days to Come, The Little Foxes, Watch on the Rhine*. New York: Modern Library, 1942.

Inge, William Motler. *Four Plays: Come Back, Little Sheba, Picnic, Bus Stop, The Dark at the Top of the Stairs*. New York: Random House, 1958.

Jones, LeRoi. *Dutchman and The Slave: Two Plays*. New York: Morrow, 1964.

Kaufman, George S. and Moss Hart. *Six Plays by Kaufman and Hart*. New York: Modern Library, 1942.

Kaufman, George S. and Morrie Ryskind. *Of Thee I Sing*. New York: Knopf, 1932.

Kelly, G. "The Show-off." *Representative American Dramas: National and Local*. Eds. Montrose J. Moses and Joseph W. Krutch. Boston: Little, Brown and Co., 1941.

Kopit, Arthur L. *Oh Dad, Poor Dad, Mamma's Hung You in the Closet and I'm Feelin' So Sad*. New York: Hill and Wang, 1960.

Laurents, Arthur. "West Side Story." *Romeo and Juliet, West Side Story*. New York: Dell, 1969.

Lawrence, Jerome and Robert E. Lee. *Inherit the Wind*. New York: Random House, 1955.

McClure, Michael. *The Beard*. New York: Grove Press, 1967.

Marquand, John P. *Point of No Return*. Boston: Little, Brown and Co., 1949.

Megan, Terry. "Viet Rock." *Viet Rock and Other Plays: Four Plays*. New York: Simon & Schuster, 1967.

Miller, Arthur. *After the Fall: A Play*. New York: Viking Press, 1964.

————. *Collected Plays*. New York: Viking Press, 1957. [*All My Sons, Death of a Salesman, The Crucible, A Memory of Two Mondays, A View from the Bridge*]

————. *Incident at Vichy: A Play*. New York: Viking Press, 1965.

————. *The Price*. New York: Viking Press, 1968.

Nichols, Anne. "Abie's Irish Rose." *S.R.O.: The Most Successful Plays in the History of the American Stage.* Eds. Bennett A. Cerf and Van H. Cartmell. Garden City, N.Y.: Doubleday, Doran, 1944.

Odets, Clifford. *Six Plays.* New York: Modern Library, 1939.

O'Hara, John. *Five Plays.* New York: Random House, 1961.

O'Neill, Eugene. *Ah, Wilderness! and Two Other Plays.* New York: Modern Library, 1964. [*All God's Chillun Got Wings, Beyond the Horizon*]

————. *Long Day's Journey into Night.* New Haven: Yale, 1956.

————. *Plays.* 3 Vols. New York: Random House, 1954.

————. *Three Plays.* New York: Modern Library, 1959. [*Desire Under the Elms, Strange Interlude, Mourning Becomes Electra*]

Owens, Rochelle. "Futz." *Futz and What Came After.* New York: Random House, 1968.

Rice, Elmer. "Street Scene." *Twenty-five Best Plays of the Modern American Theatre: Early Series.* Ed. John Gassner. New York: Crown, 1969.

Saroyan, William. *The Time of Your Life and Other Plays.* New York: Bantam Books, 1967. [*My Heart's in the Highlands, Love's Old Sweet Song, The Beautiful People, Hello Out There*]

van Itallie, Jean-Claude. *America Hurrah.* New York: Coward-McCann, 1967. [*Interview, TV, Motel*]

Vidal, Gore. *The Best Man.* New York: Dramatists Play Service, Inc., 1962.

Weidman, Jerome and George Abbott. "Fiorello." *Best Plays of 1894/1899–1961/1962.* Eds. Burns Mantle et al. 1959–1960 Vol. 1 New York: Dodd, Mead, 1920–62.

Weinstein, Arnold. *Red Eye of Love: A Comedy.* New York: Grove Press, 1962.

Wilder, Thornton, N. *Three Plays: Our Town, The Skin of Our Teeth, The Matchmaker.* New York: Harper, 1957.

Williams, Tennessee. *The Glass Menagerie.* New York: New Directions, 1945.

————. *A Streetcar Named Desire.* New York: New Directions, 1947.

General Collections

Bullins, Ed, ed. *New Plays from the Black Theatre*. New York: Bantam Books, 1969.

Clurman, Harold, ed. *Famous American Plays of the 1930's*. New York: Dell, 1959.

Couch, William, ed. *New Black Playwrights: An Anthology*. Baton Rouge, La.: State University Press, 1968.

Gassner, John, ed. *Best American Plays: Fifth Series 1957–1963*. New York: Crown, 1968.

———, ed. *Best American Plays: Fourth Series 1951–1957*. New York: Crown, 1968.

———, ed. *Best American Plays: Supplementary Volume 1918–1958*. New York: Crown, 1968.

———, ed. *Best American Plays: Third Series 1945–1951*. New York: Crown, 1952.

———, ed. *Best Plays of the Modern American Theatre: Second Series 1943–1946*. New York: Crown, 1945.

———, ed. *Twenty Best Plays of the Modern American Theatre 1930–1939*. New York: Crown, 1939.

———, ed. *Twenty-five Best Plays of the Modern American Theatre: Early Series*. New York: Crown, 1949.

Halline, Allan G., ed. *Six Modern American Plays*. New York: Modern Library, 1951. [*The Emperor Jones*, O'Neill; *Winterset*, Anderson; *The Man Who Came to Dinner*, Kaufman and Hart; *The Little Foxes*, Hellman; *The Glass Menagerie*, Williams; *Mister Roberts*, Heggen and Logan]

Parone, Edward, ed. *New Theatre in America*. New York: Dell, 1965.

Critical Studies

ON ARTHUR MILLER

Murray, Edward. *Arthur Miller: Dramatist*. New York: Ungar, 1967.

Welland, Dennis. *Arthur Miller*. New York: Grove, 1961.

ON EUGENE O'NEILL

Cargill, Oscar, N. Bryllion Fagin, and William J. Fisher, eds.

O'Neill and His Plays. New York: New York University Press, 1961.

Gassner, John, ed. *O'Neill: A Collection of Critical Essays.* Englewood Cliffs, N. J.: Prentice-Hall, 1964.

Gelb, Arthur and Barbara. *O'Neill.* New York: Harper, 1962.

Miller, Jordan Y., ed. *Playwright's Progress: O'Neill and the Critics.* Chicago: Scott, Foresman, 1965.

Raleigh, John Henry. *The Plays of Eugene O'Neill.* Carbondale and Edwardsville, Ill.: Southern Illinois University Press, 1965.

General

Abel, Lionel. *Metatheatre: A New View of Dramatic Form.* New York: Hill and Wang, 1963.

Abramson, Doris E. *Negro Playwrights in the American Theatre: 1925–1959.* New York: Columbia University Press, 1969.

Atkinson, Justin Brooks. *Broadway.* New York: Macmillan, 1970.

Bentley, Eric Russell. *The Dramatic Event: An American Chronicle.* New York: Horizon Press, 1954.

Blau, Herbert. *The Impossible Theater: A Manifesto.* New York: Macmillan, 1964.

Bond, Frederick W. *The Negro and the Drama.* College Park, Md.: McGrath Publishing Co., 1969.

Brustein, Robert Sanford. *Seasons of Discontent: Dramatic Opinions 1959–1965.* New York: Simon & Schuster, 1965.
———. *The Theatre of Revolt.* Boston: Little, Brown, and Co., 1964.
———. *The Third Theatre.* New York: Knopf, 1969.

Clurman, Harold. *The Fervent Years: The Story of the Group Theatre and the Thirties.* New York: Knopf, 1945.
———. *Lies Like Truth: Theatre Reviews and Essays.* New York: Macmillan, 1958.
———. *The Naked Image: Observations on the Modern Theatre.* New York: Macmillan, 1966.

Downer, Alan S., ed. *American Drama and Its Critics.* Chicago and London: University of Chicago, 1965.

Freedman, Morris. "The Real Molly Goldberg." *Commentary*, 21 (April 1956), 359–65.

Gassner, John. *Dramatic Soundings: Evaluations and Retractions Culled from 30 Years of Dramatic Criticism*. New York: Crown Publishers, 1968.

Kerr, Walter. *Pieces at Eight*. New York: Simon & Schuster, 1957.

———. *The Theater in Spite of Itself*. New York: Simon & Schuster, 1963.

———. *Thirty Plays Hath November: Pain and Pleasure in the Contemporary Theater*. New York: Simon & Schuster, 1969.

Krutch, Joseph Wood. *The American Drama Since 1918: An Informal History*. New York: George Braziller, 1957.

McCarthy, Mary. *Theatre Chronicles: 1937–1962*. New York: Noonday, 1963.

Meserve, Walter, ed. *Discussions of Modern American Drama*. Boston: Heath, 1965.

Nathan, George Jean. *Passing Judgements*. Rutherford, N. J.: Fairleigh Dickinson University Press, 1970.

———. *The Theatre in the Fifties*. New York: Knopf, 1953.

Tynan, Kenneth. *Curtains*. New York: Atheneum, 1961.

Weales, Gerald C. *American Drama Since World War II*. New York: Harcourt, Brace & World, 1962.

———. *The Jumping-off Place: American Drama in the 1960's*. New York: Macmillan, 1969.

Young, Stark. *Immortal Shadows: A Book of Dramatic Criticism*. New York: Charles Scribner's Sons, 1948.

Index

Abel, Lionel, 16, 88, 91, 92, 96, 97
—*Metatheatre*, 88
Abe Lincoln in Illinois, 118
Abie's Irish Rose, 81–82
Adding Machine, 86. *See also* Rice, Elmer
Admirable Crichton, The, 3
After Strange Gods, 34. *See also* Eliot, T. S.
After the Fall: familial context, 43, 52; social, familial, and personal guilt, 46, 47; autobiographical import, 51; Miller's interiors of experience, 53; fantasy needs fulfilled, 54; "symbol," 58; is "clinical," 80; Senecanism in, 97. *See also* Miller, Arthur
Ah, Wilderness!: compared to *Our Town*, 20; discussed, 22; mentioned, 21
Albee, Edward: in search for new forms, 10; confusions of, 12; one-act plays of, 77–78; Jewish depictions of, 83; compared to Inge, 86; success of, 89–90, 93; Senecan practices, 98, 102; grotesqueries of, 119
—*The American Dream*, 78, 83, 93, 98–99, 122; *The Death of Bessie Smith*, 78; *The Sandbox*, 78; *Tiny Alice*, 102; *Who's Afraid of Virginia Woolf?* 78, 89, 91,

99; *The Zoo Story*, 11, 78, 122
All My Sons: in the style of Ibsen, 10; guilt aspect in, 43, 44, 45, 48; discussed, 48–49; Miller's interiors of experience, 53; a curiosity, 54; "symbol," 58; moral ambivalence, 85; criminality, 85. *See also* Miller, Arthur
American Drama and Its Critics (ed. Alan S. Downer), 89
American Dream, The, 78, 83, 93, 98–122. *See also* Albee, Edward
American Hurrah, 103
"Amos 'n' Andy," 88
Anderson, Maxwell, 19, 82. *See also* Stallings, Laurence
—*Winterset*, 61
Anna Christie, 9, 22, 25. *See also* O'Neill, Eugene
Annie Get Your Gun, 125
Anouilh, Jean, 77, 109
—*Antigone*, 109
Apartment, The, 71
Arendt, Hannah, 38
Aristophanes: quoted, 2; mentioned, 107
—*Lysistrata*, 107
Artaud, Antonin, 100
Atkinson, Brooks, 6
Auntie Mame, 68
Awake and Sing, 48, 51, 78, 83. *See also* Odets, Clifford